# Desperately Dating

## KC Shomler

Bonfire Books Press

# Contents

Dedicated to the lonely, the lovelorn, and the brokenhearted.

It gets better.

I promise.

I am deeply grateful to my amazing stepson, Zac Shomler, for prodding me out of my comfort zone to co-host the Desperately Dating Podcast. We had so much fun together! Along the way I realized I had some useful things to say about dating and relationships. This book would not have happened without that experience with you, Zac.

Thank you.

# Introduction

Finding true love *is* possible. I am proof of this.

My husband likes to tease me by pointing out that I went on about 8,000 dates in my quest to eventually find him, and he's not all that far off. It was actually closer to 30 or 40, but who's counting? *Everyone* is counting, that's who! Otherwise, why would you have picked up this book, if not to learn the secrets to finding true love? You very possibly have an (un)impressive number of entries racked up on your dating card, too. (No judgement—that's how the game is played.)

Because here's a not-so-secret secret: dating is a numbers game. That means that you have to get your shit together, go on enough (read: lots of) dates, keep learning and growing, and resist settling down too soon. And you, too, will find a soul-satisfying relationship. I am a firm believer that there is someone out there for each of us and it is never too late for love. Love may not appear on our desired timetable and can be damned elusive. If you can manage to keep your heart open and persist with good intentions, chances are you will find who you are looking for.

Sounds simple, right? Well, it can be—if we avoid getting in our own way.

I'll tell you the story of how I did it. How I "desperately dated" in an effort to not feel so pathetic after my divorce. How I overcame the shame and embarrassment of being single in my 40s and took time to heal and learn and grow from it. This allowed me to finally see the myths about dating and relationships that had been holding me back from finding (and staying happy with) Mr. Right. Throughout this book, I'll be sharing a sample of these dates and the insights I gained so that you can gawk, laugh at my foibles, and possibly see a bit of yourself in them. And maybe—hopefully—learn something useful.

The quest for love wasn't necessarily an easy process for me, but neither was it hard. It just required time and effort. The cool thing is that all that time and effort helped me grow as a person, regardless of my relationship status. Read on and you'll see what I mean.

First off, let's begin with an eternal question: what even *is* love and why do we need or want it in our lives? Our parents and seeing how they interacted with each other was likely the first introduction many of us had to what "love" means (for better or for worse, depending upon what we witnessed!). Were the people who raised us kind and respectful toward each other? Did they smile a lot and seem generally happy? If so, that's what we end up expecting love to be. But if they were acrimonious and nasty to each other with tense silences but stayed together (or split up), then that becomes our early—and possibly lifelong—understanding of how love works. These patterns become ingrained and we tend to not be aware of or question them. Not everyone is raised in a two-person household, but I'll wager that most of us have some early exposure to love relationships between adults that leaves a mark (or perhaps a scar).

Society tells us that love, the romantic kind of love, is an essential element for a complete life, but the details after that become somewhat hazy. Depending upon where you get your information on such matters, love is an act of fate—a random lightning bolt shooting out of the sky and knocking you silly when you finally meet your person. Others portray love as a complicated calculation in which we weigh a person's faults against their assets and determine whether they're a suitable match. Many confuse love with lust or affection, or even simple kindness. Some of us want love to heal us where we hurt. Or complete us where we're lacking. Some want love for companionship or security or even status. If any of those ring true for you, then this likely isn't the book for you.

Because this book isn't a step-by-step guide or a paint-by-numbers manual with how to get a guy or a girl or a they in ten days or less. This is my story of searching for real, true love. The kind that makes you swoon but also challenges you to be a better person and never stop growing. I won't be preachy about it, but I do think that there's valuable information within these pages for those of like minds on the love quest.

So just relax and enjoy the story. You'll find that I'm a concise writer, but I'll also put a summary at the end sharing my dating methods and all the little bits of wisdom I gleaned along the way for those who prefer the shorter version.

Now—back to love and what I believe it to mean. Love is about allowing myself to be truly naked in front of another person and not holding back who I am. It's being seen on a deep, profound level—understood and accepted and even admired for who I am. (This can be hard to receive, or at least it was for me and maybe even still is, but I'm getting there). And it means giving exactly that back to the other person (and it's always way easier to give). Creating a judgment-free zone in our relationship where it's safe for us both to learn and grow, as well as explore the world and ourselves. It's about having a wingman for the inevitable hard times in life, someone who won't abandon me when things get a little tough (or when I myself get a little tough). Love is also about celebrating the joys in life together, small and large. Cheering each other on through it all. Laughing together so hard that your cheeks hurt. Much is made about fireworks and passion when talking about love, but don't confuse those things for love (although sure, there's gotta be some heat between you for it to be a satisfying relationship). I won't fill this book with a bunch of salacious details, but will admit that I'm unapologetically sex-positive. Sex is nothing to be ashamed of and can be a great source of joy, but physical stuff can't be the only glue holding you together, because it won't.

I'm partial to this as a definition of love by John Wellwood, American psychotherapist and author:

"When we reveal ourselves to our partner and find that this brings healing rather than harm, we make an important discovery—that intimate relationship can provide a sanctuary from the world of facades, a sacred space where we can be ourselves as we are ...This kind of unmasking—speaking our truth, sharing our inner struggles, and revealing our raw edges—is sacred activity [that] allows two souls to meet and touch more deeply."

Maybe it's time for a bit of a disclaimer. I'm not a matchmaker or a therapist or any kind of scientist who studies romance. My own experience in love and relationships is the only real qualification I have to write this book, but luckily, I think that's the only one that matters. I've found true love, and so this makes me an expert. Right? Okay, not really. But I am observant and have experience and wisdom from which to draw upon, and I gleefully pass those things on to you here.

You'd think that dating is merely about getting to know the other person and evaluating them as a potential romantic partner. While this is true, I found what I learned about *myself* through dating much more enlightening and ultimately helpful in the search for love. I thought I had it all figured out when I resumed dating after divorce, but no—no indeed I did not.

I did do *some* things right, though—I took some time alone after the breakup, I cried, I reflected, I owned my part in the failure of my relationship, and then I made a detailed list of everything I wanted (and wouldn't tolerate) in my next relationship. Healed and whole once again, I dove back into the dating pool. If only it were that simple.

I was *far* from healed from the ending of my marriage when I first started dating again. But even though it goes against conventional wisdom, I do believe that dating helped heal my broken heart. It was through exposure to lots of different people via dates—lots of them—that I identified the parts of me that were still broken and hurting. Tending to these wounds allowed me to get to know myself better, and a complete picture of what was important to me in a partner and relationship started to fully emerge. My initial list was a helpful starting point, but lived experience through dating was what allowed me to refine the sketch, so to speak, of my longed-for love.

That said, true love didn't just show up one day and bite me in the ass. However, with a little thought, a little time, and a little patience, it got a lot easier to find my way in the dating world (you'll see what I mean by this in a bit).

It also bears a mention that I'm a consummate introvert, and so if *I* can successfully navigate dating and find a great relationship, surely you can, too. It was scary and uncomfortable in the beginning, putting myself out there and meeting a lot of strangers. I was way, *way* outside my comfort zone. But once I made it through the nerve-racking first few dates, gained a little confidence, and figured out my dating routine, it started to feel easier. This might not sound very romantic, but compare this with job interviews or public speaking—it really does help to practice. And online dating is kind of a dream for introverts, if you think about it. You get to shop for a partner online, quietly and privately. You can be whoever you want while chatting virtually, so go ahead and try on some bolder sides of yourself. It's a low step into the online dating world for the more introverted amongst us, but just make sure that you don't stay there! It's so important that your cyber canoodling becomes a real-life date soon. A big tip for my fellow introverts is to look for another introvert who understands your temperament and doesn't want to change it. To be honest, I've yet to meet an extroverted person who understands and accepts that we're okay the way we are—introversion and introspection and all. Your real love will love you for *all* of you, not despite certain parts that they grudgingly accept, tolerate or even secretly plot to change. Remember that.

But I don't mean to exclude the lovelorn extroverts—there's plenty of solid wisdom here for you within these chapters, too! But I do think that most of you find meeting and talking with new people a whole lot easier than the rest of us, and in that sense, you've already got a leg up.

I'm writing this book about relationships with my single friends in mind (including you)—past, present, *and* future (because I hate to break it to you, but many of your current relationships aren't gonna make it, for one reason or another). Also, bear in mind that I'm a woman who loves men, and so that's my perspective within this book. Does that mean my experiences and the advice gleaned from them don't apply to other genders or relationships? I don't think so. I believe that in as many ways as we are different, so are we the same.

# Breakups Are Hell (and Other Lies)

♥

Why am I starting off a book about finding true love with a section on breakups? Because in my experience, breakups are the beginning of new relationships, or at least most of them. Unless you've never, ever had a relationship before (bless your heart, truly) or if you've been involved in, ahem, concurrent relationships, something new follows when something else ends.

So no—breakups aren't *all* bad. In hindsight, my divorce was actually great for me. More on that one later, but I've found that breaking up invariably means that you weren't meant to be together. I've outgrown all that "if only…" bullshit about timing and potential and maturity—if it isn't right for one of you right now, it isn't right for either of you right now, and very possibly ever. Better to move on and save the both of you some heartache.

I'm also vehemently opposed to the whole "break-up and make-up" cycle, even though I became trapped in it myself on more than one occasion. That shit *never* works. If you have reason enough to break up once, the handwriting is already on the wall. You're just choosing not to see it (and unnecessarily torturing yourself). I speak from experience. It can be a hard choice at the time to break up forever, but it'll be much harder the further you go down the emotionally battered road with the wrong person. Just let it end.

And letting it end can be exciting! It sure was for me. Painful initially to be sure, but ultimately *much* better for me. Had I stayed in my unsatisfying marriage, I'd never have grown so much personally, met so many interesting people on dates, or—eventually—found the love of my life. That breakup hell was so very worth going through in exchange for what I have now, which is so far and above what I thought was possible in a romantic relationship. I assumed that there'd always be compromise and hard work and conflict and subjugating myself and my needs in service to making the relationship work. Because that's kinda what we're taught, right? We're led to believe by societal attitudes and the truly frightening number of relationship fix-it books on the market that relationships are *hard.*

And maybe they are hard simply because we don't fit together.

Maybe we find someone attractive, but they have a worrying lack of ability to take care of themselves as a grown adult. Or they say they value family, but then spend very little with their own and give you a hard time when you want to be with yours. Perhaps you have great sex, but no deep emotional connection. Or they are big on romantic gestures, but in heated arguments treat you like shit. Let's say they make a lot of money, but are stingy or have a pesky gambling problem. You want to spend money on experiences, they want to collect material goods. If you are doing complicated computations such as these, weighing pros and cons, trying to decide if you want to get into or stay in a relationship with someone, then the answer is no. A great fit will feel like an easy yes.

Think of the best friends in your life, the ones that "get you" on a deep level. You talk for hours, finish each other's sentences, can tune into each other's moods, feel peaceful when together and laugh til you cry at the same stuff. You have fun together but can also be "deep". If you don't know what I mean, then you need new friends! But seriously, you feel like yourself and you like who you are with people that "fit" with you. You may roll your eyes at each other once in a while, but for the most part, it is easy and fulfilling. Romantic relationships can feel like this too, honest. A good fit ensures that there will be ease with your partner without significant compromise. I'm not saying no compromise, but it will be relatively painless. A good fit will feel easy – not because it requires no effort, but because the effort won't feel burdensome. You also won't feel like you need to keep score to make sure you aren't being ripped off by this person, because you will know at a basic level that they are committed to you and the relationship just as much as you are. I know it may seem idealistic, but it really is possible.

My husband Steven and I are an example of how being compatible on many levels makes for a great fit. We are both creative introverts, we love books, music and food, have experience with grief, hail from the same generation and are cat people (even though we currently have a dog). I could go on, but I think you get the picture that in major and minor ways we complement each other. In fact, my husband and I are such a great fit that our relationship feels effortless (even though it isn't). I don't dread conflict anymore because we're both kind individuals at heart, so we communicate lovingly and can talk about hard stuff. When we do happen to get it wrong from time to time—because we're only human—we give each other grace and we repair it immediately. And you may roll your eyes because the next part sounds so incredibly cheesy, but he *really* is my best friend. I know, I know...it sounds like what you're "supposed" to say about your spouse, but I truly feel this way. When I have important news to share or problems to process or a funny story to tell, he's the first one I seek out. I have a dear friend who goes on lots of "girls trips" with her friends, and I just can't relate. If I have time off and am going on a fun adventure somewhere, I want it to be with him.

But first, more on breakups, because it's so important to get this right. How you process a breakup absolutely affects the energy you bring to your dating and relationship path thereafter. It's hard enough moving on when things end badly. Somebody lies or cheats, or has an addiction that they can't beat or is abusive, or abandons you in a time of great need—whatever it is, that undeniably "bad" thing sort of helps us get over the person we're leaving behind. There's a good, clear reason why we're splitting, which makes us feel self-righteous and gives us a much-needed boost of strength to move on.

But how about when it's a less dramatic, slower death of a relationship? Growing apart and falling out of love and all that bullshit? In my experience, that's harder to get over even though it seems less fiery and more benign. But it's insidious; it sneaks up on you when you're not looking and then you finally wake up one day and realize that your relationship is dead. Or you don't, and you continue to soldier on in mediocrity because you have so much shared history and, maybe, couches. Or kids. Or both. You rationalize to yourself that things aren't that bad even though they could be better. Your relationship isn't a failure but neither is it a success, and things just aren't bad enough to go through the pain and hassle of a split.

That was me. That's my story right there.

Even when you feel confident in your decision to split up, there'll be some rough waters and challenging feelings ahead. I found it useful after my divorce to have a counselor to help me process all that muck while navigating it. Friends and family were helpful here too (sometimes), but a professional, uninvolved third party allowed me to be transparent about everything without fear of judgment from the people I see regularly. It helped me make sense of what went wrong, what went right, and what I could learn from my marriage to come back even stronger.

For the record, no matter the reason for a breakup, being a jerk to your ex will *not* make you feel better in the long run. It may be satisfying in the short term—an eye for an eye and all that—but it won't feel good to you inside to harbor that anger and hold that grudge. Be classy about it. Especially, *especially* if you have kids involved. They don't miss a trick, so be mindful of what you're teaching them about how to human. Also, be cognizant of the fact that even though you think your ex is a total fuck-up who done you wrong in the worst way, that's still your child's parent you're talking about. It's in everyone's best interests to maintain those parent-child relationships going forward, so don't say awful things to each other or about each other on the way out the door. Hurting them isn't going to help you feel better, nor will stalking them on social media or badmouthing them to all your friends. Well, maybe a little of that can be medicinal, but not too much—it'll just keep the icky energy flowing around you, and that prevents you from healing and moving on from the relationship.

I believe that it's necessary to stay single for a while to improve your chances of finding true, lasting love. Take some time to reflect on your failed relationship and figure out what you can learn about yourself from it and what growing you need to do. Yes, *you*. I may be getting a little preachy here, but this is hard-won experience I'm sharing with you, so listen up: it may seem like the entire fault with the relationship rests with the other person, but this is rarely 100% true. Is your "picker" really broken, or do you have some inner wounds that lead to bad choices? Are you always a sucker for a pretty face and a black heart? Can't seem to resist "bad boys" who treat you like absolute crap? Always falling for someone's potential self but not who they are right now? Explore why these patterns exist for you and you'll grow where you need to most.

But what if you weren't the problem in the relationship and it really *was* all that jerk's fault? You still need to process those emotions and figure out how to move on. Holding onto the hurt does you no favors, so don't underestimate the value of grieving the loss. Nobody in their right mind wants to do this, because it's awful and hurts like hell. But it's necessary to allow time and space for the ugly crying, hurt feelings, disappointment, and other yuck to wash through you.

I made myself really sit with that pain of a broken heart and failed marriage. I knew from previous experience with grieving that avoiding the loss, covering it up, lashing out to replace hurt with anger, or trying to numb it out is *never* going to work. That said, some semi-spirited ex-bashing with my friends and family did feel therapeutic in the early days of our separation, but I knew that carrying on with that brought the risk of me becoming a dried-up, bitter old spinster. The angry divorcee isn't exactly a good look to prospective partners, either. I went on plenty of dates with guys that couldn't seem to resist bringing up their exes and how angry they still were toward them. Bit of a turn-off there. I think that it's better to cry, scream, run for miles, feel like shit, write bad poetry, throw darts at pictures of your ex, or listen to sad songs on repeat—whatever helps you process the pain. This is how you dispel the hurt so that it doesn't turn into a bitterness that poisons your soul and repels new love. Essentially, it's how you let that shit go.

Even though it was hard to move past my self-righteous hurt and anger, I chose to be kind to myself, feel the pain, and grieve it so that I could fully let my ex go. This was the only way to effectively move on with my life instead of getting stuck in the pain of the past. And, for good measure, I wished him well. Truly—even when he was still pissing me off—because he's the father of my kids, and so it really is beneficial to me for him to find happiness. A happy dad is a better dad to my children, and they're my biggest priority. Even if I didn't benefit from his happiness in this direct way, I would still wish him well because that's the right thing to do. I loved him once and will probably always care about him. We weren't happy together at the end, so why would I begrudge him finding that happiness elsewhere? More happy humans in the world is better for everyone.

But please, I implore you, don't rush to couple back up with somebody else! I thought I was ready for a new relationship *far* earlier than I actually was, but this was just a desperate move to fill the new void in my life and make myself feel better. It didn't work for me and chances are it won't work for you, either. And remember—your friends and family (and kids, if you have them) have to go along for that ride too, so be careful what you're signing everyone up for. You certainly don't have to be celibate, and you can date for fun if you're up to it. Just don't lock anything down (or let them meet your family, especially your kids!) while you're still healing. It's just too soon.

There are plenty of good, solid, and emotionally sound peo-ple out there to date, but you need to earn your place in their ranks. Healthy people attract healthy people, so don't neglect your own self-improvement efforts. Healing takes time.

I know that I'm still healing nine years after my divorce. I feel pretty good on the daily, but stuff still pops up even now that takes me back to my painful past. Case in point: I recently had someone come into my work life that sent me right back to who I used to be in a painful, previous relationship.

I've become aware—through much self-reflection, reading, contemplation, and a healthy dose of therapy—that I have trouble with angry people. It tweaks something from way back and makes me feel off balance, unsettled, and highly anxious. And yet I went into a meeting with an angry colleague that I knew was going to be challenging, armed with my hard-won defenses locked and loaded. I thought I was prepared, but I still struggled mightily. Despite my best efforts to maintain my calm inner balance, I was pushed off the cliff and into a familiar old sea of anxiety and unrest.

I found myself thrashing about and throwing out conciliatory lifelines to this angry person at work, just like I used to do with an old ex. It was like everything I learned from my previous experience went out the window. I reverted right back, trapped where I used to be, trying to appease an angry person—a person who was triggered by me bringing up valid concerns and intent on blaming me for everything wrong. And, just like back then, my body reacted. I felt the rising, suffocating well of anxiety in my throat, my heart beating fast, my hands shaking, and my speech pressured and speeding up to the point where I felt like I was choking on my words. That feeling took two days to fully subside, painfully reminding me how I used to live with it on a daily basis for years. I don't know how I survived that experience looking back. It felt incredibly damaging.

Even though I thought that I was long over being vulnerable to angry people, this experience at work showed me that I still have healing to do and room to grow. At times of stress when defenses are low, those rotten old patterns can still come roaring back. I feel ashamed that I lost my inner Zen, because I treasure it so deeply—especially after so many years living in a relationship that was the opposite experience of that. This was a cue for me to regroup and remind myself that someone's anger is *their* problem, not mine, and that it probably isn't going to be a productive conversation anyway if anger is present. It might be best to try to connect again later. Also, it's okay for me to bring up stuff, even challenging stuff. I'm kind about it, so if the other person doesn't want to hear it, so be it. It isn't my responsibility to fix the situation for them or make them feel better because they're angry and out of control—that's *also* on them. It's up to them to grow or not, just as it's up to me to recognize where my responsibility ends and theirs begins.

I bring up this sordid work tale to remind everyone that healing from old relationships is a process and takes time—often more time than you might think. It may also continue to crop up occasionally and cause misery. All of us are works in progress in this life. But stay peaceful and focused on healing and growing from these challenging remnants of old relationships. Things *do* get better. Even though I was thrown off balance by that encounter with the angry co-worker, it was an excellent reminder of how far I've come and how much better my life is without that angry ex who used to make my life hell. Good job, me!

No way around it: breakups are hard. Even when they're clear-cut, easy decisions and a long time coming. The fallout tends to drag out for a bit and can be a riot of shifting emotions, sometimes even taking years to fully subside. Stay strong. If something big enough comes along (or builds up) to trigger a breakup, listen to it and don't go back to that person. We get lonely, we think they've changed, that we've changed, the situation has changed, or the timing is better, but we're wrong. Your mind—or maybe your heart—is fucking with you by trying to restore balance in your love life. This is a common pattern, but have you ever seen it work out? I've seen it, I've done it, and...no—it has never, *ever* worked out. Be strong and move the fuck on. Keep yourself single for something better—don't keep rehashing the past. Give the wound the time it needs to heal and err on the side of more rather than less time for this. How do I know all these gems of wisdom to be true?

Because I did the opposite. And I paid the price.

# *My Divorce*

♥

I began my "desperately dating" phase far too quickly after my separation from my first husband. And yes, that's "separation," not "divorce." I feel incredibly sheepish telling on myself with this story, but hey—it's for your benefit.

But maybe some context before we unwrap that little painful nugget.

In my younger years, like most others my age then, I didn't "date" in the usual sense of a means to meet new guys and check out their romantic qualifications. Back in my day, we'd meet potential partners through friends, at school, or at work. If there was mutual "like," then boom—we were "in a relationship." Sometimes short, sometimes long, but definitely exclusive and, in my mind anyway, headed for marriage (sooner or later). Why waste time on non-marriage material? I knew I wanted the traditional picture of a romance, a wedding, some kids, and a settled future. I was nothing if not goal-oriented!

Despite this vision for my future, I was kind of a late bloomer really and barely dated in high school. This was in contrast to some of my young adult peers who exhibited early "desperately dating" tendencies, moving from one relationship to the next without even a gap for air. I just wasn't that interested. I was more into my friends, killing it at school and getting into my dream college. I didn't experience my first (puppy) love until I was 17, almost 18. It was a dreamy summer of love but over and done by the time I started college.

Ahhh, college. I did end up getting into my dream school (UC Berkeley) and there commenced one of the happiest times of my life. Good friends, good school and good weather—much appreciated after growing up in the grey and rainy Pacific Northwest. Plus, my older, favorite brother lived in nearby San Francisco with his cute baby and absolute doll of a wife. It was a treat to spend time with them while finding my feet as a newly semi-independent person.

I still didn't date much. A little dabble here and there, but for most of my college years I was coupled up with my first serious boyfriend. In retrospect, we were a terrible fit together! But at the time, it made sense. We were part of the same friend group and that was enough for a relationship back then. We were together for 2 years during a time in our lives when neither of us really knew who we were ourselves. We broke up during vacation, on a night train between Berlin and Prague and I remember feeling distraught about losing so much shared history. It felt like such a waste to let it all go. Like walking away from a bad investment— it feels wrong but is actually the best thing to do. Quit spending time or money in places that don't serve you well. Wish I could say I learned that lesson then, for good, but I didn't.

After college, I had another two-year relationship in my 20s with another poorly-fitting guy. He was cute and a talented artist, but we did not see the world the same way. I was on a goal-oriented track to a (doomed) career in medicine and he was into his art without much thought of the future. Our paths did not align.

Still having only rare dates throughout my 20s, I was more into my friends and getting though nursing school and graduate school. Luckily though, I was patient when it came to love. Well, at least before I hit 30. I've always been happy in my own company and blessed with a solid social circle, so I didn't feel the need to be coupled up all the time. I remained unattached the majority of my adult years before getting married at 32. There were some dates and minor associations, but nothing very meaningful or long-lasting. Which seems weird given how set I was on getting married, but I was picky—even back then.

Then I met my future husband. He was dorky-cute, with sparkly eyes and midwestern sensibilities. After flirting for a couple of weeks at work, he asked me out on a date. This felt different to me—more grownup, like a traditional date. Kinda like how it's portrayed in movies. I said yes.

I dithered about what to wear, as you'd imagine, settling on a summer outfit that felt cute but didn't seem like I was trying too hard. He picked me up at my apartment in downtown Seattle and off we went. Fast. He had a sportscar that he was very proud of then, but I was car-clueless so his car pride was lost on me. There was an easy walk at a waterfront park, Mexican food in Fremont, and then we went back to his place—no, not for what you're thinking—to see his house renovation projects and listen to a little guitar (cringey, I know). No hanky panky. Then he drove me home and walked me to my apartment door, up all four flights (I was thinking, *I could get used to this chivalry!*). We said goodnight, and just as I was closing the door, he reached for my waist and pulled me toward him, saying "Not so fast," and then laid a great kiss on me. I felt like I was in a rom-com! Floating on air, I shut the door and did the little smile and semi-swoon thing that feels so unlike pragmatic me. It was surprisingly fun!

More dates followed. Holding hands all over Seattle, we saw live shows, ate lots of great food, and drank our way through the budding craft beer scene. Hikes and walks and talks and plenty of travel. There was great chemistry. We did sneaky, naughty things at work, laughed a lot, and had fun. Things were light but nice. He met my family and I met his. We went camping and survived a solid week of rain in a tent in the San Juan islands. I marveled at the fact that I could spend extended amounts of time with him and not tire of his company (this was a new feeling to me—usually I'd start craving alone time after a day or so of togetherness). We also worked on his house together, which was me mainly ogling him in his tool belt. But still, I was there, perhaps holding a paintbrush.

But then two things happened that signaled trouble in paradise. And if I'd been paying even an *ounce* of attention, I wouldn't have missed them.

One day, something made me sad—I don't remember what exactly—and I was crying to him over the phone. He drove over to comfort me, which was just what I needed but would have never asked for. I felt so loved and cherished and was really in deep smit from that act of pure care. However, when I was weeping over the phone with him again sometime later (I wasn't a frequent crier or anything, not that there's anything wrong with that; these were rare tears), he didn't come. In fact, he made it clear I shouldn't expect that type of response from him, saying that he didn't want me to get used to him coming whenever I needed him. I was too stunned to respond. Or maybe this rang a familiar bell inside me from childhood—the idea that I was somehow too much work and that it was my responsibility to comfort myself. This was the first stop sign I rolled right on through with him, but there were more to come.

Sometime later, we went on our first big trip together. Basking in the Hawaiian sun, we played at the beach, had spicy sex, and drank far too many cheap Mai Tais at the hotel bar. We weren't all alone, though. His best friend and his sister both lived on the island, which meant that we naturally also spent a lot of time with them. Being an introvert, "peopling" takes a toll on me, especially with new people (even though I didn't have this framework to understand this about myself back then). Well into the trip, after one particularly full day of "peopling," I couldn't hide my disappointment when we received an invitation to stop by the friend's house just as we were finally headed back to our hotel. This situation sparked our first full-blown argument. In his view, I was just being selfish and making life difficult for him, keeping him from his friends. In my view, I'd been spending a *ton* of time with a bunch of new people and was ready for a little break to recharge. I mean, *I* was on vacation, too, so give me a break! I think I eventually apologized just so that the tension would ease (I wasn't very adept at navigating conflict back then). But, looking back, I believe that these two incidents cemented our roles in a relationship that would struggle along for another 15 years after that fateful trip. He cast himself as the critic and me as the broken one in the union. It galls me to no end that I went along with this for so long!

So why did I stay? Tough to say. We did have fun together and I did like hanging out with him and there was attraction. We worked in the same field, and so that shared experience was helpful when debriefing at the end of the workday. We seemed to fit well enough. And I believed that we both wanted that idealized picture of the happy family.

What I can see now is how these two examples of our particular brand of conflict show the depth of the unhealed childhood wounds I had at that time (probably him, too, but his is not my story to tell). Back then, I hadn't yet begun to uncover the shit that I had going on underneath. Hell, I didn't even know it was *there*! On the surface, I'm sure that I appeared to have it all together—married, healthy, great career, cute kids—but below, there was a deep well of unprocessed pain that colored every aspect of my life.

Now, after all the healing I've done, I can see clearly that I accepted in my partner what my life to that point had taught me to deserve. I believed my family's story that strong emotion is an inconvenience to others and that it's best to suffer quietly and alone. Or, better yet, just take steps to ignore or numb or get over those feelings altogether. So when my husband began to treat me this way, it felt familiar—even familial. Ditto the reaction to my pitiful attempt to claim a boundary and some time to recharge after all the socializing on our Hawaii trip. I'd been taught growing up to feel ashamed of my introvert tendencies, and this was reinforced on that trip.

Extroversion was highly valued in my family, just as in most
of America. Being one who didn't enjoy the enormous, rau-
cous family gatherings; who preferred quiet, solitary pursuits;
who reveled in smaller, more intimate conversations, I didn't
exactly fit in so well. Coming from a large family (six kids)
with a giant extended family (my parents had 10 siblings
between them!), it was impossible to find much peace. I didn't
have the language then to understand that I'm an introvert
and that my behavior is *not pathologic*! I simply get tired out
and need to have some quiet time to recover after being
with people, even people I like (and I do like people!). This
doesn't make me a weirdo in the slightest (by some estimates,
introverts make up an entire third of the population), but I
kind of felt like my natural inclinations and tendencies were
looked down upon as something childish that needed to be
grown out of. When my husband took issue with my need
for space, I felt a familiar sense of shame and inadequacy,
that my temperament was a problem to be fixed and not just
who I am. It's so embarrassing and sad to write this now, but
it's true that I continued to subjugate myself in this way. I
just didn't know any better then. And so I continued with
the relationship that I'd originally thought was a perfect fit.
And it *was* a perfect fit all right—for keeping my childhood
wounds open. Of course, my husband had wounds of his
own (we all do, right?), but his were *not* up for discussion.
But this effectively kept his wounds open as well. We were
both continuing in our relationship, wracked with our own

private pain and unable to reach out to each other for comfort. Tragic.

By unspoken agreement, we kept things pretty light after those early glimpses of deeper issues between us. I was in my early 30s and was ready to settle down, and so was he. So we did. I wouldn't say that it was a deep romance at any point—except maybe for the first few months—but it worked well enough. On the surface, anyway.

We proceeded to do all the things: we picked out a cool ring, got engaged, planned a big fun wedding, and went on a fantastic honeymoon. I was holding our first baby in my arms before our first wedding anniversary. She was (and still is) perfect. Her equally amazing, smiley little brother followed exactly 18 months later, doubling our baby joy. Those first years of marriage were a total blur of diapers, lack of sleep, and mountains of laundry—all while we both worked. There was no time or space for much beyond survival parenting, and we managed to be a good team. In the beginning.

Once the fog of back-to-back pregnancies lifted and the kids became more independent, the conflict between us steadily increased. Even though we'd succeeded in bringing to life the picture of an ideal family, ours was deeply flawed. We'd committed the cardinal sin of letting our marriage die for the sake of the kids. I don't think that this is much of a rarity—it may even seem noble in a way, always putting the family first—but I am here to tell you that it's a sure path to ruin. Without regular love and nurture to feed it, our marriage, already not the strongest to begin with, withered and died. The strain of life and parenting was taking a toll, even though we had easy kids who were joys in our lives. We allowed our relationship to take a back seat to them and everything else in life—our work, the house, the yard. Beyond the obligatory fancy dinner for anniversaries or the odd night out with friends, we made no time for us as a couple. The dearth of date nights wasn't the sole reason for our failed marriage—certainly not—but it *was* symbolic of the utter lack of deep connection or effort to make our love any kind of priority.

Not a huge surprise, then, that we continued to drift apart. Likely due to my childhood hurts and fears of abandonment, I felt like the success or failure of my marriage was all up to me. Maybe if I just tried hard enough, we'd be happy and our marriage would stay intact. Unfortunately, my husband believed that this was the solution to our problems, too—I just needed to change in the ways he believed I needed to and all would be well. (How *convenient* for him!) Even though I was feeling beaten down and defeated, some small part of me *knew* that the success of a relationship takes two. If he wasn't going to do his part in making it a success, we were doomed to failure. Given this stalemate, our arguments became more frequent and more difficult to conceal. Our yuck began spilling out into the open, and every day was thick with tension until we eventually arrived at the point where we were basically roommates. And not good ones either. The love was long gone from the marriage, and I was lonelier than I'd ever felt.

I'd played the role of peacemaker up to that point, another remnant from my childhood when I used to referee my mom and dad and their sharp-edged banter that felt scary to me. But then an earthshattering event led me to drastically reorder my priorities in life. My dad and my brother Mike both died unexpectedly, three weeks apart. My world cracked—I felt raw, stripped down to my most basic core of humanity, and I was abruptly faced with my own mortality. I woke up to the fact that life was freaking unpredictable. Did I really want to spend the rest of my life putting my own wants, needs and dreams on hold while desperately trying to keep an unhappy spouse in my life? Eventually, the answer became no. It wasn't a very climactic or dramatic no, just a sad resigned I'm-not-going-to-do-this-anymore kind of no.

Fuck that noise.

I unceremoniously dumped that role, quickly. I stopped trying so hard to appease and keep the peace and resolve conflicts when they arose. I allowed the stonewalling and silent treatments to continue unchecked. I gave no fucks. I had no energy for that utter bullshit anymore. Predictably, our marriage promptly tanked.

One of my great regrets is that our kids witnessed the whole ugly demise, colored by the shock and craziness that followed the deaths of their grandpa and favorite uncle. Our lives were an insane stew of heartache and upheaval for many months, and I'm certain that this left scars on them. In hindsight, I wish that I'd protected them better, cushioned those blows, and made different decisions, but I did the best I could under the circumstances. I was admittedly far from my best—a victim myself of crushing events—but I do have deep feelings of global failure from that time. I should've and could've done better as a parent.

Would we have survived as a couple if we'd given more attention to our personal growth as individuals and to our marriage? Maybe. But I don't think we were sufficiently well-suited to each other, even if we'd been able to overcome our differences and heal our wounds. And we weren't friends. I don't think my former husband shared the paradigm that husbands and wives can and should be friends. Our marriage might've survived, but I don't think that we would've thrived in that relationship with each other, not even under the best of circumstances. We were just too different.

In any case, within a year or so of me letting go of my end of the rope, divorce was on the table.

And a few months later, still temporarily living under the same roof, I went on my first desperate date.

# Sampling the Dating Pool

♥

Why did I date while still technically married? *And* while still living with my husband? What in the world was I thinking?

I'll tell you what I was thinking, or maybe feeling is more accurate, because this clearly was not a well-reasoned decision! I was feeling unmoored, unsettled, unloved, and unlovable. My fairytale marriage had collapsed. Collapsed for good reason, but nevertheless, I had no clear view of my future anymore. I thought I was married forever—all set to raise kids together and celebrate graduations and weddings and grandkids with my husband. Retiring, traveling the world, and eventually growing old and gray together. That was all on the trash heap now, so where did that leave me?

Alone. A failure. A soon-to-be divorcee with two kids and a one-way ticket to Spinster City.

Necessary pity and grieving aside, a stubborn part of me refused to believe that love was gone from my life forever. And even though I was wise enough to recognize that I wasn't yet ready for (or even free for) a full-blown relationship, I still wanted to have a peek at what prospects were out there in dating land. Were there any good men out there? Would I be attractive to them? Could I even get a date? It may sound a little pathetic, but I was a 43-year-old woman unsure of my own value in such a youth-centric culture.

Four months into our separation, I put up a rudimentary dating profile and started looking around at who was out there in my age group or older (I'm no cougar). What I discovered was a whole sea of interesting possibilities. And the most surprising finding? I was a pretty hot commodity! Fresh meat! And why wouldn't I be? I had a lot going for me, though it's achingly sad looking back now and realizing that I couldn't see that. I needed admiration and interest from strangers to convince me that I was still attractive to the opposite sex. But that's how far down the toilet my self-esteem was at the end of my marriage. Thankfully, I've come to learn that my need for male attention wasn't pathetic at all—countless women in my situation have felt and do feel the same way. When you're feeling like used goods, damaged goods, goods that aren't good anymore, it's all too common to want to feel...well, wanted. It's a human need, after all.

Looking back, though, it was a fairly empty and surface-level attempt at boosting my spirits. Still, scanning profiles and chatting away with cute boys was an excellent lift to my mood at that time. After a few weeks of this online reconnaissance, I accepted an invitation to go out for drinks with a nice-looking Dutch man. He lived on a sailboat in San Francisco Bay upon which he liked to play his grand piano. He seemed a touch mysterious and slightly exotic.

I was ridiculously nervous, like middle-school-level freaking out. I was on the horn constantly all day with my girlfriend planning the outfit, hairstyle, shoes, and conversation topics. It was completely absurd. My anxiety shot through the roof as the appointed hour approached and I found myself pacing the parking lot of the restaurant trying to calm the fuck down.

Dutch Man eventually arrived and put me out of that misery, but swiftly catapulted me into a new kind. Bombshell to no one other than me, I guess, but people *lie* on dating profiles! I was absolutely blown away. His pictures must have been at least 10 years old—maybe 15! I still found him appealing, but the salt-and-pepper hair I'd admired in his photos? It was fully white!

Putting my shock aside, we proceeded to have a very nice, flirty, light date. He was kind and charming. My nerves calmed down after a cocktail or two, and by the end of the evening my heart rate was safely back under 100. Conversation flowed, and it felt good to have an attractive man interested in me. I felt a faint stirring of my empowerment returning. But—somewhat-predictable spoiler alert—it didn't last.

# Sucked Back In

♥

My husband was *not* happy that I'd exercised my right to go on a date under the provisions he'd insisted we establish at the time of our separation. I guess he wanted the option to date while we were still living together, but he certainly didn't want me to do the same. Throwback once again to his needs being met and not mine—and we weren't even together anymore!

There was a messy blow up the morning after the date with Dutch Man. I don't want to speculate too much on the psyche of my former husband, but I think the sudden interest in me from another man sparked some sort of deep-seated, cave-man-like possessiveness. I'll spare you the more lurid details, but let's just say that make-up sex is a thing for a reason, and it most certainly does exist.

But I didn't just cave in and go running back to him after one good tumble. No—progress had been made over the past several months that couldn't be so easily undone, and I think that he knew this. There would be parameters if we were to re-unite, one of which was going to counseling together. This was something that he'd steadfastly resisted up to that point, since *I* was the broken one, not *him*! (Cue the reg flags once again!).

But I'd be lying if I said that there wasn't a profound sense of relief on some level at the prospect of getting back together. *Ahhh, no need to go down that ugly divorce road after all. This can work out. With some effort, but at least I won't have to change course mid-life.* I wasn't immediately all the way back in on my marriage, but I was definitely headed that way. I so desperately wanted the long-pictured life with the happy ending that I turned a blind eye to all the flashing red lights trying to slow me down.

We tiptoed back toward each other, somewhat warily. Trying for a fresh start, we went backwards and started dating each other again. We found a good counselor and made some progress, but we stopped too soon. We were cocky that we'd beat the odds and successfully rekindled our love. He proposed again (in front of the kids) and I accepted. I said that it was the happiest day of my life, because that felt like the right thing to say, but I knew that those words were hollow even then. That's how bad I wanted it to work out between us, and for our little family to stay intact.

Likely an unnecessary news flash here: it didn't work out! (See above for all my warnings against getting back together after breaking up. One more time for those in the back rows—*it never works!*) It was a brisk descent back into our old dysfunctional pattern with each other. Despite my best efforts, the new communication skills we'd learned in counseling were tossed aside, and then we were in freefall with nothing to stop the crash landing that was imminent. There were some desperate attempts to slow the descent, and our marriage limped along for a bit as these things often do.

I'll never forget the moment when our spunky 10-year-old daughter, all blond curls and braces, broke into some tired old argument my husband and I were having for the millionth time to ask —why don't you just go ahead and get divorced?

And just like that, less than a year after reconciling, our deferred divorce was back on.

In retrospect, I feel incredibly guilty for dragging my two little kids along for that futile ride—getting their hopes up just to be dashed again, as well as my own. All I can say is that it can be hard to have perspective on these matters of the heart when you're in the thick of them. I have no harsh judgment for those who seemingly stay in bad relationships too long—it's a difficult decision to end something that you've dedicated years of your life to making a success and that affords us a fair amount of status in our culture. Being coupled up is sort of expected, at least in my generation. After all, there may be questions about you if you're not in a relationship. *Are you defective? Why can't you hang onto a man? What will become of you?* And so on and so forth, ad nauseum. All bullshit obviously, but those social norms are deeply ingrained and leap out at us when least expected.

Plus, we frequently get pressure—often direct—from family to "Stick it out! Don't give up too soon! Keep the family intact!" Sometimes even with a religious overtone or outright shaming. I think using terms like "failed marriage" or "failed relationship" invite feelings of shame and are horribly inaccurate characterizations of life transitions. It is more helpful to view relationships that have ended as chapters in the book of your life. Some are longer, some shorter, they may have different emotions associated with them, but all relationships end. Think about it: at some point, every relationship ends. By choice or by, well, death. Despite this truth and even though I was there insisting that my husband wasn't good for me, I believe some of my family members still wanted him to stick around. This can make things incredibly difficult and also beg the question, *Whose marriage is this, anyway?*

And then of course there's the impact of a breakup on the children. Sure, it's "easy" to stay together "for the kids". But is that really the healthiest decision? Stay together so that they can witness a dysfunctional relationship up close and learn that is what a marriage is supposed to be? No, certainly not.

But hope is strong. Hope convinces us to hang in there, even when that miniscule chance of success isn't visible with the naked eye.

The extinguishing of hope is what finally allowed me to let go of my marriage. Like water eventually eroding rock, my hope of having a successful marriage with my ex was worn down over time until it was eventually completely gone. I woke up one day and let go of the picture of the happy family that I'd been desperately grasping onto. I just let it go. Maybe like when Jack finally slid off that door into the depths of the icy Atlantic, I was resigned to my fate. I was going to be a divorcee. So be it. I'd be fine.

*Blub, blub, blub.*

# Welcome to Divorce Town

♥

E xactly two months after my husband and I had moved to a new state for a fresh start in a last-ditch effort to save our marriage, we were derailed to divorce town. Talk about disorienting! We'd just moved into an apartment to get our bearings before buying a home in the area, I'd started my first-ever teaching job, both kids were in new schools, and then *bam!* The divorce was happening. Now we had to rewrite the entire script again. Plus, my then-husband thought this would be a good time to get our daughter a new puppy. Fuck me! Of course, the doggy quickly wormed his way into our hearts to become the treasured family member that he is today, but that was just insanity. This was the *worst* time of my life. I used to think that the worst was when my dad and Mike died (just two years previously!), but no. This was *much* worse. Still horribly depleted from those deaths—plus a move to a new state, starting a new career and all the rest—adding divorce to the mix pushed me over into the abyss. I was all tapped out.

Luckily, mom mode kicked in and I focused on getting the kids and myself situated for the next stage of our lives. I wanted to make sure that I did everything I possibly could to find a new normal on my side of the equation quickly. Giving up on my marriage and accepting that it was truly over was oddly freeing. I quit worrying so much about how my life was all going to work out and just started moving ahead. Pushing forward through the fog, I was numb, but with all hope for reconciliation gone, I channeled my energy into planning my next steps. Practical yes, but also partly a distraction from the stew of emotions surrounding my divorce that burbled just below the surface. Taking care of business I could do, feeling all that shit—no way. At least not then.

It's all a blur now and I have no idea how I did it, but somehow I managed to shop for and buy a house (first time buying on my own *and* on a first-year teacher salary, both of which are no small feat). That settled, my husband and I proceeded to separate our financial lives and all our stuff while potty training the puppy and trying to keep some sense of surface normalcy for our kids.

A couple of months passed living under the same roof while preparations were made, but in separate rooms (*bad* déjà-vu from the first time). Time marked by strained family dinners together, crying by myself in the early morning before walking the dog and heading out to work while it was still dark. I was drinking wine every night back then (not copious amounts, but still not great for me, or anyone; I'm no advocate for post-breakup boozing). The drinking behavior didn't last, but my edges were so sharp at that time I took the temporary comfort afforded by the grape. Being in a new city with a new job and far from my friends, I had little support available. It was a dark and lonely time.

I realized I was going to need some people around me, at least a goddamned emergency contact for work! So I slowly started going out with work people for drinks on occasion (even when I didn't really feel it), saw more of my family that lived close by and casually befriended some other single moms in my new neighborhood. I started to feel more secure, like if I was hit by a bus, at least there would be someone to step in and watch my kids after school! I also became closer to one of my sisters during this mess. People don't really know how to relate to divorced people. It seems to make them uncomfortable in a similar way as when confronted by a death or someone's grief. But divorce is even worse, because there are no designated greeting cards to send or casseroles to deliver or formal rites of passage like a funeral to attend. It's just an end and people don't know what to do or say, and so they tend to fade away. And the hurting person hurts alone.

My sister didn't know exactly how to comfort me, but at least she recognized I had that need and stepped up. Sometimes presence is enough, and she and my brother-in-law were there for me—inviting me to dinner, providing some family time for the kids, and making me explore new parts of my new city even when all I wanted to do was curl up into a ball and cry (or die). I never contemplated suicide—my kids needed me—but I did feel overwhelmed and hopeless. Frequently.

My kids were my lifeline and reason for living, just as they'd been when I lost Mike and dad a couple of short years before. They were the reasons I kept going when everything looked dark. I'm grateful that I knew back then to expect that a new loss is likely to reactivate grief from previous losses, and sure enough, that's exactly what happened. What an absolute shit storm. In the span of two short years, the three most important men in my life were gone. There were times when it felt like more grief and sadness than one human could bear. But I did bear it. Initially for the kids but, as time went on, for myself as well.

# Hello Haven Home

♥

The sweet yellow house I found was just down the street from our shared apartment of misery. It was a high priority for me to have a stable homebase for the kids and me to recover from the divorce. With my share of the proceeds from the sale of our previous family home, I was able to afford a down payment on a cute, affordable house in a safe neighborhood. I say this bit about buying a place so casually, but at the time, this was a terrifying prospect! Being totally responsible for a home on my own felt huge and overwhelming. Financially and physically, the responsibility was all on me. For better or worse, I was pretty numb from the divorce proceedings so I just went with it in a sort of fog that blunted my tendencies toward anxiety and overthinking. Luckily, the house we found was close to school and close to the kids' dad. This location was strategic in multiple ways – trips back and forth to school for sports or for retrieving forgotten articles at my ex's house were relatively painless since the distance was not great. This made transportation back and forth relatively easy, at least in a practical sense. But emotionally? Yikes.

Having to pack up my kids and ship them off to their dad's house every few days was rough. Up to that point, I'd rarely spent even one night away from them. It felt like my heart was being torn out of my chest and I cried (privately) each time. It wasn't always smooth sailing, but I made sure they always felt loved and safe. Eventually we all adjusted.

And then I began to see how my kid-free times of solitude were actually therapeutic. An opportunity to grieve out loud and uninterrupted. There was suddenly no need to hide my tears or blunt my pain to protect the kids (I let them see a little, just not too much). And time to rest! However, gently and quietly in the background, there was a process of rediscovery happening. I began to seriously question who I was without my husband. After being a part of a couple for so long, I was at a loss for how to be a *me* and not a *we*.

I'd spent so much time in my marriage struggling to keep the waters calm, make my husband happy, and protect the kids from the strife of witnessing the slow breakdown of our marriage that I had no idea how to just "be" without all those responsibilities. For years, I felt like I couldn't relax and let my guard down—always on alert for potential danger. It was exhausting!

But I didn't recognize any of that until the moving van drove away, the front door closed, and I was all alone in my new home. The busyness of unpacking, arranging, and rearranging furniture, as well as figuring out how to get all the fucking electronics to work slowly gave way to a profound heaviness—in a *good* way, like a settling sensation into my new nest without all the constant anxiety. It eventually dawned on me that what I was feeling was peace. I didn't understand how far my life had navigated away from calm over the years until that moment. It was shocking and sobering. It dawned on me that this is how people stay in shitty relationships and other bad situations, because we adapt to it slowly over time. We come to accept—and even expect—sub-par ways of being treated. There may be things to learn from past relationships, but there is no shame in a relationship ending. I was learning that I was *so* much better than that.

Despite the ugly part of this realization, I was mostly in a state of wonder and giddiness about how much better I felt in my body. Emotionally I was still hurting, but my body was stoked by this development! I didn't feel anxious and on edge all the time, my throat was no longer constricted, and I was taking fuller and deeper breaths. I was sleeping great at night and soon had recovered enough energy to set about putting my stamp on the house that would eventually earn the name "Haven Home" (but more on that moniker later in the book).

In my marriage, my husband had taken the lead on most of the design and decoration of our homes, and I was excited now to have total creative control. Picking out furniture, changing shower heads, selecting linens, hanging art, updating cabinet hardware and faucets, painting stuff—all these tasks I could do on my own, and they were helping me find my way back to myself. The physical labor made me feel strong and independent, and the creative license made me feel a bit wild and naughty, like I was getting away with something without asking for permission. How I'd missed that side of myself!

As my space was coming together, my heart was kind of falling apart. A few months later, once everything had its place and the paint had dried, I was left with a raft of shitty feelings about my divorce to finally process. The flurry of activity couldn't permanently obscure the fact that I was alone and didn't want to be. I can say sincerely that this time around, I didn't want my husband back—we were well and truly over. Progress! But I didn't want to stay single forever, either. Or really for long at all. I still very much wanted the happy ending. The life partner. A true love story.

And so what did I do? Say it with me now, as I'm sure you've been expecting it: I dove back into the dating pool *way* too soon—again!

Some lessons are never learned. Well, until they are (but we'll get to that).

# Desperately Dating

♥

My husband and I had tried to save our marriage. We'd failed and separated—twice. We'd unlinked our physical lives (the final details of the divorce would still take some time to hammer out, as anyone who has been through it knows) and I was settling in to being just me, nobody's "missus." I found peace in the separation, but lost it once loneliness set in. I cried a lot, reviewed mistakes I'd made in my marriage, and felt hurt all over again in revisiting everything that my husband had done wrong in my eyes. I read books about divorce, watched *Under the Tuscan Sun* about 10,000 times, then decided I was over it and ready to move forward. It was the perfect time to set up a dating profile. Famous last words?

And so began my desperately dating phase. I think of desperately dating as an uncomfortable state of mind (not happy being single) that leads to unproductive actions in the search for love. I wish I knew then that I was mistaking my *desire* for a relationship for a *need* for a relationship. I wish someone had told me that a new relationship wouldn't heal me and being single wouldn't be the end of the world. My misguided mindset lead me to desperate actions to find a relationship as soon as possible to fill a lonely gap in my life.

In retrospect, it's easy to see that I was far from ready to date again. I'd only started healing and even though I don't believe any of us needs to be, or even can be perfectly whole and healthy before we start dating, I thought I was further down the road than I was. Plus, there was that goal-oriented wiring I had. Time to get out there and find L-O-V-E! I was desperate for it! And so commenced the first of many, *many* first dates.

It seemed reasonable to sign up on the Single Parents Looking for Love dating site (or some such name like that). I mean, that's who I was, right? Eager to find myself a prince, it seemed likely that a man with kids of his own would be a better fit. Someone who'd understand the demands of parenting, as well as the joys.

I picked a username (something snappy I'm sure; I'm glad I don't remember), answered the getting-to-know-you questions and dug up some pictures of myself (all awful and all dark with a strained smile—I have something akin to a photo phobia, but that's material for a different book). Hook baited, I commenced to wait for nibbles.

It didn't take long. Turns out there are a lot of lonely dads out there also looking for validation, *ooops*, I mean love. I sifted through the barrage of messages to pluck out my prince, and then I found him. Let's call him Shorty.

Shorty and I began a lengthy correspondence and it felt great! I had a real, live, adult male (single, I assumed, but internet dating made me question everything) interested in talking to me. To *me*! We commiserated on the phone about our divorces, the challenges of raising kids alone, and trying to co-parent with our exes. It honestly kind of felt like therapy. And, in a way, I guess it was. He was attractive in his photos, easy to talk to, and my heart felt light again. Could it really be this easy? Was I going to find my prince with the first horse out of the gate? Famous last words indeed!

After a few weeks or more of chatting, we eventually got around to setting a date to meet in person. Waiting for my prince in the coffee shop we'd agreed upon, I was excited. I was anxious. And I was also flabbergasted. In strolled the shortest version of 5'9" I've ever seen (I'm 5'3" on a good day, and here I was looking down on him). He was nervous, naturally, since he'd clearly *lied* in his profile and the jig was very obviously up. I tried to hide my shock and we had coffee and a bit of conversation, but it was no good. Driving away, I couldn't deny that there was no chemistry between us, even though I desperately wanted there to be. We'd been so good together on the phone and in my head! I already had us living happily ever after together! Was it just his height that had soured the deal? No, of course not—I'm not that shallow (though many men and women on dating sites appear to be). I am short and I come from a short family, so who am I to judge? Plus, I know firsthand of some amazing short men. My dad was an absolute rockstar, but probably 5'6" in shoes. He was charismatic, handsome, super smart, and successful. He was also a kind-hearted deep thinker who loved his family. But had he been single in today's mating market? He'd probably—and very unfortunately—rarely get a second look because of his height.

But back to Shorty. It was partly the deceit that had turned me off, but also the undeniable lack of chemistry. That mysterious magic or pull that makes you feel excitement deep in your nether regions was nowhere to be found. I'm no expert on what scientifically goes into creating that attraction, but I'm convinced that it's either there on day one or it's not and never will be. It wasn't just about his height—it was because I didn't feel any kind of a urge to kiss him, then or ever. Bottom line.

The date was a turning point in our budding internet romance, and not for the better. To his credit, he did ask on the phone later if I found him attractive and to my credit, I answered honestly (but kindly). Seeking to soften the blow, I offered that maybe we should go on a second date to make sure, but it never happened (thankfully). We clumsily soldiered on with our phone conversations for a while, but they were awkward and slowly petered out.

Hopes dashed for a quick resolution to my problem of being single, I did gain a lot of wisdom from my experience with Shorty.

I learned (again) that people lie on their dating profiles, in all sorts of ways. Some might be nefarious and up to no good, but I suspect that most probably pad the truth because they feel inadequate showing themselves as they are. The virtual world provides an irresistible opportunity to present ourselves as better versions. If not objectively better, than at least improved in our own minds in ways we think will make us more appealing to potential partners—taller, younger, thinner, wealthier, whatever. Most of us likely do this because, somewhere along the way, we've picked up the message that we're not quite up to the mark, and therefore somehow deficient.

The anonymity of the internet has also made people less kind in pointing out perceived flaws as well, and so there's a real danger that we'll be criticized for who knows what by who knows who. And we're tender in these spots, so we try to hide them and guard them—protecting ourselves from external attacks and internal attacks as well—those feelings of not being good enough.

So I can't really be mad at Shorty. Or the white-haired Dutch Man I dated before him. People have internal wounds that cause them to feel inferior and this leads them to lie. However, if there's no owning up to the trickery or at least acknowledging the deceit, then there'll be no second date. I'm a kind-hearted person and I understand very well how it feels to have sore spots and feelings of inadequacy. I can accept that in a partner, provided that they're open to growth in these areas. I have wounds, too—we can grow together! But if you can't even acknowledge that you shaved almost a foot off your height or a decade off your age, then I will *not* make time for you. That's a hard line that's developed for me. I'm okay with "flaws," but you need to have some measure of self-awareness that these old wounds are affecting your behavior and show a willingness to become healthier.

The other big take away from my experience with Shorty was the wisdom in meeting in person sooner than later. We kept it virtual for far too long—long enough for feelings to grow and dreams of a future together to develop. *Huge* mistake. It's a must that you meet in person early in the process to determine if there's a romantic glimmer that makes it worthwhile to continue. I believe friendship is a necessary ingredient in a true love relationship, however, there must be physical attraction as well.

Attraction will *never* grow later—of this I am convinced. I think there's something a little mystical that draws two people together in a romantic way. Or maybe it's just deeper biology—pheromones or something, I don't know—but my point is that if this part doesn't exist when you first meet them, move the fuck on. You're just wasting time.

I spent several months of my life before marriage trying to feel attracted to my best friend (we'd decided to give dating each other a shot), but I couldn't get past the oddly familial feeling I had toward him. It just wasn't there—no magnet drawing me in. But god, how I *wanted* there to be! We had a long-shared history, had fun together, laughed a ton, could talk about anything, and he was objectively incredibly attractive. But not a single goddamn spark. Nada. Zip. He did feel hot for me though, so that was uncomfortable. Sadly, our friendship didn't recover when attempting to turn back from the brink of romance and dwindled thereafter. The final crushing blow was when I met my future husband. My friend couldn't seem to accept there being a new man in my life, in the place that he wanted to occupy. He said unkind things about the doomed future of my new relationship (but hey—to his credit, he wasn't wrong), and so I let him go. I still miss having him in my life, but there was no way to move ahead for us.

When Shorty came around, the memory of that prior experience with the lack of sparks and no potential for flames cropped up again. I didn't want just a roommate or place-holder in my life—I wanted heat and passion in addition to friendship, romance and all the other things that make a relationship great. Not willing to settle, I never saw Shorty again. To be fair, another gal wouldn't have been settling for Shorty at all if they were meant to be. But Shorty was not meant to be for *me*.

So who on earth was?

# Time to Regroup

♥

After the Shorty fiasco, my confidence was shaken and I felt a need to take myself off the market and regroup. Maybe finding my person wasn't going to be as easy as I initially thought. I obviously needed more time to gear up for this finding love challenge. Not feeling ready for that kind of exertion, I took a break. I shut down my dating profile, focused more on building up my social circle, loved on my kids, and just lived my life without searching for love for a while. This was time well-spent.

The kids and I continued to work on making our house cute and cozy. It was wonderful to have a peaceful place to call home after living for so many years at the end of my marriage in a constant state of anxiety. We started having fun exploring our new neighborhood, finding all the good places to hike, eat and other fun things to do. We began traveling again, just the 3 of us. I felt good about providing a solid, stable place for my kids and I to build our new lives. The kids were doing well, making friends, adjusting to new schools and riding the school bus (a new experience for them). They felt safe and secure which allowed me to take a closer look at some of my own needs. I had taken a teaching job with a rigid schedule that wasn't working. I liked teaching, but I didn't like the inflexibility. It has always been a priority of mine to be there for my kids. I wanted to go to all the school pageants and presentations, be there to tend to them when home sick, greet them after school and feed them a snack and generally feel like I am present and involved. I couldn't really do any of those things with that job. So I changed to a position where I could schedule my own time. I know not everyone has the ability to find a job like this, but this is just one example of how I chose to make adjustments to better honor my own priorities. This made me feel more in control and not just a passive participant in my life.

However, the search for love was still working deep in the background of my mind. The cool thing was, without paying much attention, there was a lot of healing and processing going on. Doing the most mundane things like driving my car or washing the dishes, I found myself replaying parts of all my past dates, relationships, and my marriage that I liked and didn't like. My mind was on auto pilot, sorting, cataloguing, processing, and scouring through the past's useful information for future romance while I went about living my life. No active effort from me was required!

When I was ready to start dating again, I reflected about how I wanted to be and how I wanted to *feel* in my next relationship. There was a lot I still needed to figure out, but deep down, in a visceral way, all that processing of the past gave me a profound commitment that I wouldn't be settling for less than perfect. Perfect for *me*, that is. I don't expect anyone to be objectively perfect—that's just impossible (and probably boring). Humans are messy and complex and complicated; I get that and I'm okay with it. It sort of keeps things interesting. But in my post-divorce era, I was starting to realize that some things I was unwilling to compromise.

For example, I'm smart, a deep thinker and have strong opinions that I am not afraid to say out loud. I'm not a jerk about it or anything, I am a kind person, but, I know my own mind and am peacefully assertive. I see these as strengths. I've learned that not everyone else does!

There has been a particularly wide divide on this issue in my dating history. Men I've dated seemed like they were either attracted to my strength or repelled by it without much middle ground there. I've also had the experience in one long-term relationship of the guy being initially appreciative, but over time became less enthused. I guess he came to believe I was being difficult since I didn't just lay down and go along with his version of things. He attempted to shame me and make me feel like I was just too…much. That was a heartbreaking experience. And one I wasn't willing to repeat.

So what did this strong, opinionated woman to do when searching for a partner? I was intentional about finding a strong man. What does a strong man mean to me? A strong man is one who is smart, kind and secure enough in himself to be with a strong woman. A woman who has her own thoughts, might question you or disagree at times. Not for the sake of argument (although that can be fun sometimes too), but because it is important to her. To me. I also admit when I am wrong, and I might tell you when I think you have it wrong, but you do those same things for me. Kindly. Like a helpful mirror for each other. So when I was dating, I tested my dates. Might say something a little provocative here, a little opinionated there, push back in conversation and see what the response was. Some were cowed and backed down (mommy issues?) and that wasn't attractive. Some were exasperated and borderline angry (threatened, offended?) and that was unappealing and a touch scary. I needed a strong man who could keep up with me in a deep conversation and not be triggered by disagreement, but was also tender, openhearted and able to care for me when I need it and accept care from me when he needs it. Strong and soft, just like me.

I pledged that I'd have a partner who was confident in himself, even while owning his parts that still needed work (none of us is perfect, but that doesn't mean we aren't worthy of love). I'd be with someone who made me feel safe emotionally and encouraged me to keep growing into my best self. Someone who was motivated in life but didn't take himself too seriously and still knew how to have fun. There would be loads of laughter and delightful adventures. And attraction. Oh, yes—that was non-negotiable! This was my budding understanding of the concept of "fit." It was language I didn't yet have back then but would prove to be instrumental in finding true love.

These are just a few of the realizations that revealed themselves as I continued to process the past. The details became even more numerous and fleshed out as I went on to date more people. These insights were shaping my quest and would eventually lead me to a deeper understanding of what my perfect relationship would look and feel like—and it was far more detailed and nuanced than the crudely drawn picture of a happy family I let "guide" me to my first marriage.

Sound like a unicorn? Maybe. But it's hard, if not impossible, to find something when you're not specific about what you're looking for. It's like ordering a "sandwich" without any specifics and hoping that you get something you like and not that fucking gross tuna salad. You can't just set out looking for "love" without defining it and still expect to get exactly what you need and want. This is what "desperately dating" means: just flailing about out there with no idea where you are or where you're going—just ignorantly hoping that some kind of love comes along and saves you from a life of loneliness and despair. I would do better.

# Diligently Dating

♥

Americans are scrappy, goal-oriented individuals. "Hard work pays off", "good things come to those who hustle", "if you really want it, go out and get it" —sound familiar? This kind of programming tells us that we can find a partner if we just work hard enough. But love is a bit more elusive. It's like when you plant seeds; you can't make the flower bloom faster just because you want it too. You have to tend the soil, provide water and hope for enough sun but not too much, and then...wait. Similarly, you've got to do your part to set yourself up for dating success by getting healthy in yourself and making yourself available to meet people and go on plenty of dates, but then be ok with loosening your grip and letting things happen (or not). Good things come to those who are diligent in seeking love, but not desperate.

We also want what we want and we want it now. Instant gratification. Whatever happened to good things come to those who wait? Yeah, that's way out of date. No surprise people (myself included) tend to approach love and dating the same way—with impatience. Which can lead to imprudence. I should know.

The Shorty experience and all the soul searching that followed forced me to accept that finding true love was likely going to be a longer process than I'd originally thought. I refused to let this discourage me though—instead, I psyched myself up for the endeavor. I took stock of my progress: I had built a great life for me and my kids. I'd done some healing that would continue and had made a good start on my picture of my ideal man. I'd continue to refine this description to make it as detailed as possible so that I could easily spot him when he finally appeared in the dating landscape. I call this "diligently dating." It's the antithesis of "desperately dating," but has the same fun alliteration and it's worked for me.

I knew that it was a numbers game, and so I resigned myself to going on dates—lots of them. Even though I'm an introvert and the prospect of meeting a lot of new people felt dauting, I knew that I'd have to put myself out there if I really wanted this. Mr. Right was not going to walk into my house and sweep me off the couch in my ratty sweatpants (unless he's a plumber or something…hmmm, possibilities!). However, I knew I had to protect my energy so that I wouldn't completely drain my tank and give up on the whole thing, or worse, give in to an unsuitable match. I'd be no use to anyone if I was on empty—just a vacant-eyed, drooling blob. It seemed prudent to limit the number of dates to one or two per week, which felt doable. I'm a deep believer in the wisdom of enjoying whatever path you're on in life, and so I didn't want this process to be a joyless slog. I wouldn't succeed that way, as my dejected energy would surely leak out all over the place (I do *not* hide my feelings well). Plus, too goal-oriented of an attitude in dating definitely gives off desperate or mercenary energy which effectively repels the love you're seeking. I had to figure out how to adjust my mindset for this effort to protect my energy and not feel like I was living in service of too narrow a mission.

In the midst of my strategizing, I had a revelation: *this could be fun!* I was new in town and it would be nice to meet some people in the area. Yes, I was ultimately after a partner, but I didn't need to be in a hurry. My life was pretty great already—I had a good job, a cute home, and both I and my kids were happy and healthy. A man would be a bonus—not a necessity. That's an amazing feeling and a wonderful starting place for the love quest. It gives off stable, centered, self-assured vibes, which are like catnip to more evolved potential mates. You know, the ones you want to attract! At the very least, going on a series of dates would get me out of the house for some adult conversation and an opportunity to practice my dating skills.

What's the first rule of diligent dating? Be stingy with second dates! And first dates, too, now that I think of it. Having a detailed image of who you're looking for and how you want to feel in their presence will be of great help when sifting through lots and lots of online profiles. And being picky is fine—there are plenty to choose from, so there's no need to feel rushed. I turned down first dates with a creeper from my middle school years who resurfaced on the dating site (definitely *not* a time in life I'd care to revisit, like most other people), as well as an extra tall guy (6'10"!), because I just couldn't see how we would work, given that I'm 5'3". So those initial rejects are easy to identify, but saying no to a second date can be more challenging since there's a little more time invested and you might be face to face.

I definitely needed practice turning down second dates because a) I was eager to find true love—badly, and b) I had an aversion to hurting other people's feelings. Regarding a), I needed to sink more into a leisurely pace and let the process unfold. And believe my own rhetoric that there was no need for haste. With b), I needed to have a little bit more of a mercenary edge and recognize that I could trust myself to make a quick decision. Drawing it out by continuing to date people that didn't meet my criteria was not helpful to either of us. I wasn't looking for Mr. Almost Right or Mr. Right Enough—I was more than prepared to hold out for Mr. Right, full stop. And wasting time on second dates wasn't going to get me there. It *is* awkward to reject someone when they ask you out for a second date, though. It feels rude somehow. But

I found that with practice, like most things, it became more comfortable to kindly decline.

Saying no to a second date also became easier as I began to trust my instincts rather than overthinking it (like I usually did). If it wasn't an unqualified yes to seeing that person again, then it was a no. That's it—no need to justify it, no messing around. It also helped me to remember that I didn't have to force a connection, as there were plenty of guys out there available for dates. Scarcity didn't have to be a concern! I was happy in my life, and so I could take my time searching for the *real* Mr. Right. Interesting, that idea—being mercenary enough to keep moving forward in the quest but not so much so that you repel what you're trying to find. Because nobody likes to feel like they're being hunted or interviewed for a job on a date. A delicate balance to be sure, but I found that it definitely wasn't impossible. How did I do? Read on!

# Mr. Streamer

♥

Armed with new energy, insights, and strategy, I was ready to take on the dating scene again. Since going online seems to be the only viable way to meet enough men to support success, I set up a new profile.

And yes—before you say it, it can be argued that it's better to meet someone with whom you already have some kind of direct connection (work colleague, checker at the grocery store, fellow gym rat) or indirect connection (friend of a friend, someone's brother or cousin, dog walker). I say that it might be worthwhile to leave the door open for these potential sources of dates, but they have their drawbacks, too. At best, they're probably sporadic producers of potential mates. To avoid the scarcity mentality, you need a large pool to pick from. And what if you date a co-worker or someone else in your life that you see regularly and it doesn't work out? Awkward. Or what if a helpful friend sets you up and the guy is a turd, but your friend is *sure* that you're destined to be together? It can be hard to let your friend down easy that there will be no further dates with whomever they've presented you with. I've experienced "the set-up" more than once, and *none* of them worked out. It's mystifying to me why these matchmaking friends thought that we'd be well-suited. *Do they really know me? Or him? Or are we just two random, single people in their life that they decided to push at each other?* Nope, the dating sites are a much better hunting ground in my opinion—lots to choose from and, equally important, separate from friends and family who'd love to get involved with your love life. I'm sure they mean well but are ultimately best left out of the process.

When it comes to choosing a particular dating site, I honestly don't think it matters which one you use. I've tried a few of them and didn't notice much difference in the quality of matches in my target demographic. As long as there are plenty of prospects available that meet your criteria, I don't think that any one platform has a clear advantage. Maybe the cost is a factor or the user interface is better on one of them or other stuff, but go ahead and pick one and get swiping or winking or whatever. Just make contact!

*Lots* of contact. (To be clear—I'm referring to finger-to-screen contact at this point.) I kept front of mind that meeting many guys would increase my chances of finding Mr. Right. This time around, however, I took a little more care with my profile than I did with my "sad sack single parent" efforts. I thoughtfully answered the getting-to-know-you questions, carefully crafted my statement about myself and what I was looking for even though it seems like photos are the main thing most people use to determine interest. I think I mentioned previously my aversion to having my photo taken and my resentment of some of the sexist bullshit that happens on dating websites, however, I did post my best, most recent pictures. Including full body shots since so many men seem hyper-fixated on body size. The common euphemism I often saw was a desire for women who are "height and weight proportionate." (Whatever that means!)

I could go on and on about how shallow men (and women) are and how unfair it is to judge people solely on their appearance, but physical attraction is not negotiable. If it is not present, for whatever reason, it won't be a good fit. Unless, of course, you're looking for an asexual relationship. I think that most of us want some heat though, so you might as well put out there what you really look like—not the professional headshots you had done 10 years and 50 pounds ago. Shallow? Yes, people are. Me? I'm just telling it how it is. And take heart, because what people find attractive is vast and wide-ranging. There will be someone who thinks you are gorgeous and amazing as you are right now. Trust.

So I accept some of the more odious (to me) parts of playing the game, but I do have my own personal bullshit limits. Take, for example, the guy I chatted up who was cute and who seemed interesting and intelligent. He had photos of himself taken mid-stride while running and was obviously quite fit. During our first chat, he pressed me for details of my health and fitness regimen. I mean like *granular level* details. What would be next? A scheduled weigh-in and body fat percentage assessment while he fine-tunes my nutrition and training schedule? I tried making a joke about it, but he was dead serious. I'm a healthy person and I do take care of myself, but this was a no just on principle. The last thing I'd want in a partner is someone who was rigid about his wellness and judgmental about mine. Fuck that. I eat tofu and do yoga, but I also drink martinis and binge Netflix at times. I need balance. So *that* guy didn't even get a first date.

But the truck driver who told me funny jokes did. He was attractive in a burly, hirsute, masculine way (I'm a sucker for that). We started a fun, bantering chat, and he made me laugh. Remembering the importance of meeting in person soon, I moved us toward a date and he picked the spot.

A bar and grill—solid pick, nothing objectionable, and thoughtfully mid-range driving distance between us. I felt less nervous for this date, thanks to recent dating experience informing me of what to expect and a less desperate outlook. *There are plenty of prospects out there, and I need not be in a rush, so let's see what happens with this guy.*

He was a big, cute galoot. I could tell that he was nervous though, and our initial in-person conversation was halting at best. I hoped that the drinks would lube us up, but before we'd even ordered, he whipped out his phone and commenced showing me a series of funny YouTube videos he liked. Okay, one or maybe even two to break the ice would've been fine, but there didn't seem to be any end in sight to this. Each time one ended, I sat up and turned to him ready to start talking. And each time he just cued up the next thing he wanted to show me. How long can you paste on a smile and feign interest in a series of inane videos? For me, that answer was one date.

And what was the takeaway from this encounter with YouTube Guy? I *need* conversation. I know—I go on and on about how I'm an introvert and how much I like being alone, but not while I'm with someone! I can be a downright chatterbox in the right company. And I love talking about deep questions (I have a philosophy degree after all) and shallow politics and hopes and dreams and whatever. My man needs to be able to keep up, not hide behind a barrage of stupid cat videos.

So YouTube Guy, yes—you were a big, cute galoot. Just not the galoot for me. I trust that you and your YouTube Gal have met and are happy in silly video bliss!

# Sexy Bald Guy #1

♥

I've never ever had sex on a first date. Not a badge of honor or anything—just a statement of fact. But with this guy, I must say that I was *really* tempted.

Clearly an experienced dater, he suggested a meetup very quickly after mutual interest was expressed online. I proposed that we meet for drinks as I'd come to feel comfortable with cocktails for first dates. It was a short time commitment in case the date was painful and yet long enough to get a sense of any potential. Plus, cocktails are a fun social lubricant, ideal for an introvert like me. He agreed and we picked a place with outdoor seating in our mutual hometown. It was a glorious sunny summer evening.

Okay, he was attractive in his photos, but in person? *Damn.* Tall, solidly built, rocking the bald look, he was casually but elegantly dressed. And he smelled amazing. There was some serious heat coming off that man. Judging from his smoldering gaze, the feeling was apparently mutual. I'd never experienced anything like that before—an instantaneous, animal attraction to a stranger. It was honestly kind of freaky, since I tend to be more of an in-my-head type of person. But I liked it.

Conversation was light and easy and before I knew it, I'd sucked down two martinis (I'm usually one and done). Pleasantly tipsy and randy, we decided to walk about the cute little downtown area. He took my hand to gallantly help me stand up and pulled me in for a juicy kiss (I can just feel my kids cringing reading this!). Totally slick move—and I was there for it.

We walked and held hands and stopped every block or so to kiss some more. Intensity steadily increased. I'm not sure where the time went, but it eventually got dark outside. We'd walked and smooched throughout the entire downtown area and then made it back to my car where we proceeded to lock lips some more. He asked me if I'd give him a ride home. The question had the same effect on me as a bucket of cold water to the face. *Oh, wait a minute—this is a not-so-subtle invitation to take this fit of passion to the next level at his place.* My brain was instantly back online in her prim and proper pajamas (it was way past my bedtime anyway) telling me "no way." My body, however, was seriously considering it! *This is new and interesting territory...maybe I can just do it for the experience...*

Nope. My brain is strong and swiftly talked me out of it: *You don't know anything about this guy. What if he's a killer? Or into weird sex stuff? Also, you don't really have the best lingerie on for this…*

I wasn't trying to be a tease, but I'm sure he felt that way when I politely declined to give him a ride, in my car or otherwise. Half-hearted plans to get together again were discussed after that steamy night, but never happened, and eventually conversation trickled to a stop. Kind of a bummer, but that's how it goes sometimes.

So what did I learn from this sexy beast?

That instant attraction is real! Maybe I was ovulating or the moon was full or he was in his werewolf phase, but the desire was unmistakable. The other thing I learned was that I'm not cut out for hookups. In retrospect, I can see that he was most certainly on the prowl and looking to get laid from the start. Nothing wrong with that, but it's just not who I am. I still wanted the perfect picture—I wanted true love. And this guy didn't seem interested in going much deeper than my cleavage. So just like I'd said no to Shorty with whom there was zero physical attraction, so too I dispatched Sexy Bald Guy # 1 (there'd come to be more Sexy Bald Guys down the road—stay tuned) who had it in spades, but not much else. I could've had a little dalliance with him just for kicks, but it ultimately felt like a waste of time on my search for Mr. Right.

And so the quest continued.

# From Dumper to Dumpee

I don't mean this to sound cocky, but I didn't have a lot of familiarity with rejection. In relationships up until that point, I was the dumper most of the time—or at least the decision to end things was mutual. I didn't have an extensive dating history, so maybe that explains the lack of experience being spurned. But all that was about to change.

He was intelligent, quick-witted, and had the kind of long hair that was popular in the early 90s while I was in college that still caught my eye. That style sometimes looks a little dirtbag-ish—especially when combined with a flannel—but nevertheless, I found it appealing. We met for happy hour at a random hotel bar—an Embassy Suites or something similar. Classy! I guess it was a convenient place close to his office where he liked to go for drinks with co-workers. I was game and showed up looking cute.

From the very start, he seemed a bit disinterested. I amped up the charm offensive, flashing a lot of teeth, flicking a lot of hair and making loads of clever remarks. By the end of the date, I still thought he was interesting and was open to a second date, but he declined. And, helpfully, he provided me with the stock phrase I'd end up co-opting for future use: "I'm just not feeling a connection, but it was nice to meet you."

*Huh. Well, this is new.*

I drove home in a thoughtful daze. Reviewing the date in my mind, I searched for any slip-ups or gaffes that might explain this unexpected turn of events. Did I have toilet paper stuck to my shoe or spinach in my teeth? Did I misjudge his political affiliations and make some offensive remarks? Is my laugh weird?

It's sad and telling that my first impulse was to look for what was wrong with *me* as the reason why he didn't want a second date. Probably not an unusual response, but still, kind of pathetic. At least I sure felt that way.

Further reflection led me to acknowledge my wounded feelings instead of trying to shame myself out of them. No way around it—being passed over hurts. Maybe not to a devastating degree, as not much was invested yet, but there's still a sting. And this honest acknowledgment gave way to even more significant realizations and reaffirmations to carry forward with me: Sometimes the spark just isn't there and it's not because one of you is defective.

I comforted my bruised ego with the knowledge that there are many potential mates out there, so there's no need to settle if you or he don't feel it. Just keep looking. But perhaps most importantly, follow this man's example and be kind when rebuffing someone, because being turned down doesn't feel good. That's why I loved and stole his brush-off words. They were direct, succinct, and not something that could be argued with. Not feeling a connection gets the point across without leading anyone on or leaving the door open (as some less well-designed rebuffing lines can inadvertently do).

I personally believe that giving a detailed explanation of why you don't find someone attractive is *not* helpful—even if they ask for it. I say this for a number of reasons. First, it's fucking messy. Do you really want to have that kind of intimate and potentially damaging conversation with someone you barely know? I mean, what if they get defensive (or worse)? Second, it's not your place to critique a person you barely know. They need to figure out their own shit.

And finally, who's to say that they aren't a perfect fit for someone else out there? Just because they don't ring your bell doesn't mean that they're beyond salvage. Keep it kind and keep putting positive energy out there. That's precisely how you attract the same back to you.

# Roll Out the Red Carpet

♥

M y dating methods were becoming well-honed by this
point. I had a go-to outfit (cute and flattering dress), a
set routine (drinks at a quiet, local cocktail bar), reliable conversation ideas, and a well-coined phrase for turning down a
second date. I was *not* prepared to be outmaneuvered!

He was a bit older—maybe even a tad on the too-old-for-me
side—but I was keeping an open mind. He also lived far away,
so that was another strike against him, but he seemed eager
to drive in my direction, so what the hell? At the very least, it
could be a fun night out and more experience with the dating
process. I also liked that he rode a Harley. What can I say? I
have eclectic tastes! (In men and all other things, really, but
that's neither here nor there.)

Well, color me shocked when this guy flipped the script on me and literally rolled out a tiny red carpet on the table when I arrived. I'm not even kidding—an actual, mini red carpet fashioned out of felt. (Plenty worn and matted-up, too, so I knew that I wasn't the first date to receive this treatment. If this bit were a traditional pick-up line, it would be walking with a cane and collecting Social Security by now.) He also ceremoniously presented me with a bottle of his homemade blackberry wine. There are few things I like less than sweet wines, but one of them is being played. This is part of the reason why I detest car salesmen, realtors, and solicitors at my door (and I doubly detest the latter for the invasion of my protected, introvert space). I don't enjoy feeling like someone is trying to manipulate or sell me on something. It just gets my hackles up.

Caught unawares by this move, I felt off balance. *Where's this date going?* Apparently, he'd arrived at the bar early and already forged a bond with the waiter, with whom he proceeded to have an in-depth and ongoing conversation as I sat right there in front of them, largely ignored. I'm not exaggerating—I felt like a third wheel on my own date! I was out of there so fast, but not before I'd slugged down my drink and shoved that awful jug of wine in my purse. I'd fucking *earned* that bottle! (Too bad it was terrible—better suited for topping pancakes than anything else.) I didn't even feel bad for being borderline rude. *Abrupt* is probably more accurate but, in any case, I didn't feel a need to make this guy feel better about acting like a jerk. Maybe this was how he coped with his first date nerves, but I wasn't about to stick around and find out.

The atrocious wine ended up down the drain, as did any hopes Mr. Red Carpet may have had of seeing me ever again. Maybe he and the waiter continued *their* relationship, heaven knows. The lesson here: save the pomp and circumstance for Oscar night—*not* a first date.

# Morrissey Has Entered the Building

I t was the hair that attracted me. For a goth-adjacent girl who grew up in the 1980s, Morrissey was *everything* and his hair is unmistakable. Look it up if you need to—it's important hairstory I mean history. (Sorry—I made myself groan with that one.) So, naturally, when I saw a profile of a guy who strongly resembled Moz, I was intrigued. Turned out that he was also a book lover, intelligent (these two things often go hand in hand), and easy to talk to. I decided to overlook the fact that he seemed to capitalize on the Morrissey resemblance a little too much, and we agreed to meet at the quiet cocktail bar I had on heavy rotation for first dates. (They were getting to know me there by now. *"That poor woman…here again. When will she ever learn?"*)

He couldn't meet until later in the evening, and so the bar was noisier than my usual happy-hour meetups. Live music was playing and it wasn't really an ideal situation for conversation. But it was still a ton of fun! The band was swingin', the drinks were flowing, and I was getting lost in Morrissey's eyes as we vibed to the music. As we were leaving, I impulsively asked him to kiss me after such a magical night. He did, and it was a nice little peck. We both walked away smiling.

The next day we were making plans for a second date. My first second date! This felt momentous! He suggested a taqueria with good margaritas to be followed by a whiskey bar. I'm not much for brown liquor, but I adore tacos and I loved that he had such a well-thought-out plan. It feels good when someone takes the time and care to put something together.

I wore a sexy dress and was ready for a night of revelry. This dating thing was kind of fun! He was looking delicious and was very chivalrous. I love it when guys take the lead and order for me and bring me drinks. I don't think that I'm high maintenance and I certainly don't expect these little niceties, but I'm always impressed and appreciative when they occur.

More, deeper kissing at the end of the night—but sadly, not as good. Toward the bad side of the spectrum, to be honest. That was a bit of a disappointment, but the sparkling conversation and genuine fun we had together made me willing to look beyond that. Kissing can be taught, right? I absolutely *did* find him attractive so perhaps the, ahem, romantic side of things could be, well…refined. A little hint of desperation on my part there looking back, but what can I say? I liked him and was definitely game for a third date.

But here's where things got weird. He'd been eager for another date at the end of the second—we both were. As luck would have it, though, he was in the process of moving and so it would have to be delayed. No problem on my end—I was in no hurry and our online conversation was as good as ever. But in hindsight, I see now that he was starting to lay down some hints at having reservations about distance and other factors. We did live on opposite ends of the city with a bridge between us, and his move would take him even further in the other direction. His kids were quite a bit younger than mine too, so they weren't exactly well-matched regarding activities and interests were we to bring them together. I think that in the end, the math simply didn't add up for him to want to continue seeing me. But here's the thing: he never actually *said* that. It was just a series of excuses and postponements, and I was too dim to pick up on the hints. I tend to take people at their word and not question their motivations. I like direct communication. I can handle it if you don't want to keep seeing me, so just spit it out! It took an embarrassingly long time for me to catch on, but it was a learning opportunity.

I've thought a lot about why people choose to communicate in this way in the dating scene. It would be easy to chalk it up to cowardice, or maybe even sometimes cruelty or callousness. Perhaps a general avoidance of anything that might be potentially messy emotionally. What I prefer and choose to believe is that most people don't want to hurt anyone's feelings. This is why they ghost you or let the budding relationship fade rather than speaking their minds. Maybe I'm being overly generous here, but the story I tell myself can either reflect well on humanity or not. I choose to see the good. And maybe making the choice to give someone the benefit of the doubt opens me up for being taken advantage of, but I'd prefer to err on the side of being too trusting than the opposite.

I also think that many people have shockingly low emotional intelligence and social skills. Unless you're lucky enough to have parents who value interpersonal skills and can teach you, how the hell do you learn this stuff? If nobody guides you to consider another person's feelings and to do right by them, even when you have other options that would be easier on you, chances are that you'll take the path of least resistance. It's hard to let someone down, but it's possible to do it kindly. Also, wrapping things up cleanly and clearly in this way is better for everyone—the dumpee can stop wondering if they're going to call and the dumper can feel good about doing the right thing.

# Rocker Feller

♥

This guy looked like he stepped right out of the pages of *Hit Parader* magazine (it's an 80s reference, so look it up if it's gone over your head). Long—much too long—stringy, dirty blond hair. Wispy chin beard. Skinny, sinewy build, but strong. Tight jeans and a rock T-shirt of questionable cleanliness. Perfect! I'm kidding, but here's a little-known fact: Iron Maiden was my first-ever concert experience, so I do have some heavy metal running through my veins. Plus, I'm an equal opportunity dater! But seriously, how did I pick this guy? Well, how do you pick *any* guy from a sea of possibilities on dating apps?

I think that many people make the mistake of picking based on shit that doesn't fucking matter at all. Example: many women set their filters to exclude any guy under six feet tall. Women like tall guys, and I'm not going to even begin to tackle why this is a thing, but just know that it is. I've got the same bias in fact, and I don't even really understand it.

Plus, I'm short, so why does it even matter? However, do you have any idea what proportion of American adult males is over 6 feet tall? About 10%, according to data from the CDC website. The same source reports that the average height of adult men in this country is 5'9" and the average for adult females is 5'3". So why are we excluding so much of the dating pool in favor of gaining a few inches? I'm all for being detailed in building the picture of the mate you're looking for, but this seems inane. Are those three *vertical* inches really going to do a better job of keeping you warm at night? Of encouraging you in life, of laughing with you, of comforting you when you're sad, of engaging you in deep, meaningful conversations? I think not.

What criteria *really* matters? For me, I had a long list of needs, wants, and wishes for my ideal guy. Some of it was non-negotiable (must be kind, smart, motivated), some was whimsical (similar music tastes, quirkiness), and some was just, *"It would be nice, but I'm not going to turn someone down if they don't have it, provided they check many other boxes"* (like tall (!), dark, handsome, and hairy). I didn't formally rank these different criteria against each other, but I did have more of a working sense of what was more important to me. For instance, I'd take kind over rich and successful any day of the damn week. Fortunes come and go, but somebody kind at your side *will* keep you warm at night. I believe that genuine kindness and compassion are the true and much too rare gems.

How to apply your carefully curated partner criteria to the snippets and pictures you get in dating profiles? You can't. Dating profiles are a crapshoot at best, as people lie and misrepresent themselves and post old pictures. One way I tried to suss out good prospects was to look at how many of the getting-to-know-you questions they answered and how thoughtful their responses were. The profiles that only have pictures and short or flippant words don't tell you much of anything helpful about that person, except maybe that they aren't serious about dating. And, sometimes, offer a glimpse of a dark soul—not gonna lie. Such vitriol and misogyny! I also vehemently dislike and caution against filling your profile with a tiresome list of negatives. Why would you try to attract someone by detailing, ad nauseum, everything you *don't* want in a partner? Let's see—you don't want a woman with kids, or curves or a mind of her own? Well, dang it, guess I'm not gonna be a fit for you. But those duds are easy to spot and avoid. Pictures are useful, since physical attraction is important, but they're also an inefficient means to find a mate just on their own. If you base your selection only on how they look, it'll probably take many more dates to find the right person—and perhaps increase the possibility that you burnout on dating, settle for the pretty face, and regret it later.

For me, the picture might've stopped the scroll, but then the real detective work began. Do they express themselves well? Do I get a sense of their personality, and do I like what I'm reading? Do they have a brain and are willing to use it?

This is definitely a must in my book, because I like full and wide conversation. By the way, intelligent is *not* the same as educated—they're entirely two separate things. Someone can be super smart without having any special, expensive letters behind their name. I also observe how they come across while chatting. Do they seem engaged or too cool to show interest? I'm a straight shooter and I like to tell it like it is. Someone who's veiled about their feelings or playing ridiculous games about how many days to wait before contacting me and other stupid shit like that is *not* going to win my heart. Who has time or patience for that?

So, back to rocker feller. What was it about him that made me reach out and go on a date with him? Well, aside from his appearance (which I didn't find wholly unattractive but was perhaps a little outside of my usual tastes), he was clearly a good guy. He also had a little something offbeat about him that I found interesting—he played in a band (of course) but also taught middle school music, and it was obvious that he loved those kids. Heart melt. I surmised that he was likely kind and patient if he'd chosen to become a teacher, since people don't tend to just fall into that profession. I find teachers attractive because it suggests not only a generous, helping personality but also some sense of being driven by a higher moral purpose. Nobody goes into education looking to get rich! They do it because they believe in the mission, and this is very appealing. As was his intelligent conversation and desire to talk about a broad range of topics. For me, that's like catnip! First impressions: definitely dateable.

We met at a divey bar he chose because it had a great jukebox. Fine by me. We spent an hour or so talking about bands and music and concerts. I felt a little bit like I was back in high school, but it was enjoyable. He seemed more than a touch nervous and unsure of himself, saying at one point something about how I couldn't possibly want to see him again. *Huh?* I was having fun and would've happily spent more time with him, but not if he's gonna try and talk me out of it! I find that sort of unkindness to the self off-putting. I know that many see self-deprecation as a valid form of humor, but I just don't like it. I don't like cocky either, but when people say mean things about themselves, I flinch inside. Probably because my dad did this to the extreme while I was growing up, and it always made me feel bad to see him beating himself down. How we talk to and about ourselves matters. If you call yourself a loser and assume that someone couldn't possibly like you and want a second date, well, you're basically speaking that into existence. And in this case, that's exactly what happened with Rocker Feller.

Shame, really, because I could see myself really liking him. But if you're not liking *yourself*, then you're letting me know that there's not really all that much for me to go crazy over.

# Sexy Bald Guy #2

♥

I'd been diligently dating for about six months and had learned a lot about myself and dating and people in general. I'd also managed to remain focused and avoid coupling up too soon with unsuitable people. My dating skills were better and more efficient—I developed a feel for how to pick solid prospects out of a lineup, I had my trusty go-to outfit and place to meet for dates, and I'd practiced saying no to second dates so much that it felt easy(ish) to do in a kind and clear manner. All that focused energy and attention, and meeting new people was still fucking exhausting! I was plum worn out. And then I met Sexy Bald Guy #2.

He was a couple of years older and worked in healthcare but not in a clinical role, so we did speak the same language and understand each other's careers to some extent. He was a great conversationalist, able to veer from literature and philosophy to politics and rock music without batting an eye. He'd grown up overseas due to his father's career and had some interesting stories to tell about going to high school in South America as the only white guy. Fluent in Spanish—very sexy! Again, not my usual physical type, but he had a captivating smile with dimples and nice eyes. Kind of smoldering eyes, actually, and there was definitely some heat between us.

This may seem self-serving, but I needed a break from dating and didn't really want to be all alone. I'd come to enjoy going out a couple of times per week for adult conversation and a little romance. Sexy Bald Guy #2 and I had been on a couple of dates. He was charming and cute, and so we embarked on a light and not at all serious romance. More of a flirtation, really, but we were enjoying it. It was a relief to put the search for love on hold and just enjoy the companionship. I didn't have a name for it back then, but in hindsight, he was my first Mr. Right Now. A pleasant interlude, but not Mr. Right material.

He was a little old school and treated me well—took me to fun new restaurants and out for drinks, for walks at the waterfront, and on adventures to surrounding quaint towns for sightseeing. He made me feel attractive and sexy. It was fun and I leaned into it. I even had him meet my sister and brother-in-law one night a few months in, since it seemed like he was going to be in my life for a while. Until...

I don't really remember why or how it came out—maybe some kind of hint from something he said—but I began to suspect that he'd lied to me about his age. We were now in the Google era, and so I started researching him. Maybe I should've done that earlier in the game, but I'm fundamentally a trusting person. Anyway, LinkedIn proved me right—he'd shaved 10 years off his age (unless he graduated college at age 12). What the fuck? Ten years? That's not a wee stretching of the truth—that's a decade!

Affronted by this information, I'm embarrassed to admit that I ghosted him. I should've confronted him, but I was so shocked and bewildered that I didn't. I stopped communicating—just shut it down with no explanation given. Very immature. Shame on me.

This was a rude awakening—that even a guy I'd been seeing regularly for a few months could be so boldly deceitful. Disheartened and sobered that I could fall for such trickery, I retreated from my romantic quest to lick my wounds in private. I knew that I needed to spend some time feeling bad about this. Feeling betrayed and foolish and ridiculous. Nobody likes feeling like they've had one put over on them, me included. That's weird though, right? It's the *other* person acting shitty, so why do we, the victims, feel bad about ourselves for being duped? But we do. In any case, I took some time to work through those feelings because I knew that I didn't want this one guy's boneheaded move to sour me on the entire male species. The last thing I needed was the story in my head that no one can be trusted. I knew in my heart that there were plenty of good guys out there who don't lie about their age or otherwise misrepresent themselves, who feel comfortable in their owns skins despite their imperfections—advancing age or height or balding scalps. Whatever it is they feel tender about, I knew that there were plenty of men out there who could manage those feelings without trying to save face at the expense of their integrity.

I'd find myself one of *those* guys.

# Fish Farm Guy

♥

After a much-needed break to recover my equilibrium, I started flirting with Fish Farm Guy. Talk about geeky cute! He was actually some sort of high-level environmental scientist who worked with area fish hatcheries. He'd relocated from somewhere deep in the Midwest and lived in a small town about an hour away. He did remind me in many ways of my first husband—cornfed white boy with a big brain, nice eyes, and a funny sense of humor. I usually go for a little of an edgier type, but his wholesomeness was appealing in a way. He felt steady and dependable. I know that may sound boring, but there's comfort there for someone like me who has easily activated anxiety. Being around people with good energy and a calm presence is deeply soothing.

Chatting with him was easy and light—he had a fun, quick wit. We set a date for afternoon patio beers outside at a cute bar. He was smiley and a bit nervous in person. But the beers soon worked their magic, and we were happily gabbing away in no time. So what does one talk about with an environmental scientist? Gardening! We shared what we were both growing in our summer yards...he built fences to keep the deer out...I just accepted their presence and propensity for eating my roses as part of the natural cycle of life—benign chatter like that. But I could sense that he was holding something back. Not about the garden, but something else he really wanted to talk about. And a couple of beers in, it eventually came out: did I have any retirement savings?

Well, *that's* an odd thing to ask on a first date.

Curiosity piqued, I had to know where this line of questioning was coming from. As it turned out, Fish Farm Guy had some complaints! His experience with dating was that the majority of women he'd been seeing lacked financial stability and had nothing saved for retirement. This made him feel like he was seen as simply a meal ticket, and he didn't want the burden of supporting another person in a relationship. He was getting very animated and self-righteous about this, and he was losing his appeal by the minute.

To be fair, he obviously had a wound there.

I can appreciate his point of view; having attitudes about money that mesh is an important factor in any relationship. Yet it still felt rather grim and distasteful. Maybe I was stung on behalf of womankind—don't lump us all together and don't draw conclusions about our abilities to be fiscally responsible without knowledge of the reasons why one might not have a healthy savings put away. And don't forget—we still make far less than you for the same work, and so it takes us longer to save similar amounts. I could go on, but you get what I'm saying here—women put up with a lot of bullshit and glass ceilings and all the rest, and so you might want to give us half a break, Bozo. And don't draw conclusions about our character or potential as a partner based on the number of dollars we have put away. (Obviously, I have a wound here, too).

My other objections are more idealistic. I believe in love and marriage as a true joining of two lives. Being together means sharing a home and a family. And money. To do anything else feels the opposite of committed. Perhaps transactional, even. I know that plenty of people are far more businesslike when it comes to the money side of love and marriage, and they work very hard to separate the two. But I believe in *love*. I mean, it says it right there in the vows—the richer and poorer stuff. Fish Farm Guy's perspective also seemed blatantly hypocritical—he didn't like being judged by the size of his bank account but turns around and does exactly the same thing. As previously mentioned, money comes and goes, but do you like the person underneath? *That's* what's more important and what lasts. Money doesn't fix character flaws, it just obscures them.

And another gripe I have is that nowhere in our required education in this country are we taught about saving for retirement. So unless you're lucky enough to have a mentor in your life who makes sure that you start your retirement savings early, maximize your employer matching funds, and take advantage of compound interest over time, how the fuck are you supposed to learn that stuff? Plenty of people—men and women—are very capable of creating a financial plan for retirement; it's not that hard. But often, you don't know what you don't know, so it's unfair and unwise to draw conclusions about someone's value as a person based on the size of their nest egg. They may not know how to go about saving or investing, or they could be terrible at managing money, or have a predilection for risky investments, or harbor an ugly gambling habit. Or maybe, maybe, they had a financial setback. It happens. My point is that you just don't ever know the why and if it really is a deal-breaker unless you ask. It might just be a knowledge gap or some other valid reason.

Even though this issue that Fish Farm Guy brought up stung me, the fact is that I *do* have healthy retirement, college, and emergency savings—my dad drilled the value of this into my head from a very young age and taught me how to do it. I was lucky to have his guidance, but not everyone has that. So even though I met Fish Farm Guy's criteria in the financial sense, his manner about this whole thing was a big turn off. He didn't like being dated for his money and neither did I.

Plus, he lived too far away. I tossed that fiscally preoccupied fish back into the water.

# The Burger Baron

♥

He didn't mention it in his profile, but it turns out that this guy owned a local chain of burger joints that he'd built up himself. I was fascinated by this story and attracted to his entrepreneurial spirit, and so we set up an in-person date. He suggested that we go to an out-of-the-way but very cool hilltop bar to see his friend play with his jazz band. It was a trek to get up there even though it was technically still within the city limits, but wow—what a view.

We grabbed seats at the bar, ordered drinks, and tuned into the band. They were fantastic! I'm no jazz expert, but I do love music of all kinds and was eager to talk about it with the Burger Baron. He seemed a little put out by my attempts at conversation during the set. Okay then, Mr. Grumpy Pants. During a band break, I tried again. I don't remember my exact words, but I made a comment about how cool it is that jazz has so much improvisation in it. He gave me a derisive look and—I kid you not—a snort. Then he said something to the effect of, "What? What in the hell are you talking about? That is so stupid." Well, my back immediately went up. I *loathe* being dismissed like that!

Okay. First off, who does this guy think he is? Did he know that he was being incredibly rude? Or was he just a geeky music nerd? And even if what I said was way off base (but I really don't think that it was), is that how you educate people who have a misconception? And while on a date, no less? Give me a break!

I'm sure that my feisty reaction is related to a deeper wound, so let's unpack this a little.

My husband often used to dismiss my ideas like this, too, usually when he didn't like what I was saying or when there was the possibility that I could be right and he could be wrong. It was a tactic to keep me in my place, as well as his ego intact. This was annoying, but it's just another example of his brokenness butting up against my own.

The wound goes deeper though; my reaction to offensive behavior like this is also related to how I grew up. Being the youngest of six kids, there was a lot of competition for resources such as bathroom time, food (I'm certain that this is why we all eat so fast), and attention from our parents. As a result, there was a lot of jockeying for position, "teasing," and other kinds of banter that went on amongst us. However, I can't say that it felt good natured all the time, at least not to me. It felt more like a performance in which you had to put on a good show to earn your place and some measure of respect within the clan. Maybe not even respect, actually—perhaps just recognition that you weren't a total fuck up. Mistakes, whether big or small, were not embraced or treated kindly but more often derided, in a joking manner, of course. And very often, not publicly at all—instead, these were the topics of conversations going on behind your back. Direct communication was not a big thing in my family growing up (it still isn't). But that didn't mean that you couldn't hear or feel the judgment loud and clear. This led to me being absolutely petrified of making mistakes or looking dumb or otherwise attracting negative attention. Being wrong or losing face in any way was scary, because in my kid brain, it became linked with a loss of love and acceptance in the family. It felt like there was a narrow channel to navigate in order to be deemed worthy.

So this kind of dismissive behavior brings back bad, formative memories for me. I have a tender heart and am not well-suited to the sort of brash and competitive environment I grew up in, where at any moment you could be harshly judged. I disliked that style of communication back then and I like it even less now. I don't fear being wrong like I used to—I've worked through that one—but I refuse to participate in any conversation that disrespects me and my point of view. I don't care how outlandish my ideas might be—do *not* dismiss me like you're swatting away a pest. I'm better than that.

So, needless to say, I gladly bid Burger Baron adieu. I implore you to do the same with anyone who disrespects your voice and makes you feel less than you are—even if they're in a position to supply you with free patty melts and fries for life. None of that is good for your health.

# The Mean Dad

♥

P oint blank: I can't be with someone who isn't kind to their own kids.

I met Mean Dad (what a nickname to be proud of, right?) for a glass of wine after a fairly short online chat. I wasn't immediately smitten with him from our initial interactions, but he seemed like a reasonably nice guy—and I was playing the numbers game after all—so I agreed to a date. Bad move.

It was a pretty average date to start with—typical getting-to-know-you questions and such: what do you do for work, where did you grow up, have any kids, any fun trips coming up, and so on. Simple and innocent queries, but oh, what they can reveal!

Mean Dad mentioned that he'd just returned from a trip to NYC with one of his twin sons, a trip to celebrate the kid's graduation from high school (I have no idea why it was just one of the twins and not both). This sounded promising:

a nice dad who liked to take fun trips with his kid, aware enough to celebrate the joys and milestones in life like his son's graduation. Hooray! As he began talking, I could feel myself leaning in, all prepared for the wonderful and heart-warming story that was most surely coming.

Wrong.

Instead? A litany of complaints and petty grievances that blasted me back into my seat. New York was so far to travel and so expensive, especially in the summer. The city was hot and crowded, and his son wanted to do all the "stupid" touristy stuff. And he made sure to tell the kid upfront that they wouldn't be buying any cheap plastic souvenirs or any of that "crap." What a killjoy.

All I could think was, *You poor kid! Your dad is such a dick!*

Why undertake such a trip if all you're going to do is complain about it? Was marking this milestone just another box to be checked on the parent to-do list, devoid of all actual meaningfulness and fun?

I feel like I encounter this type of parenting a lot, and parenting is something I care very much about. I'm always curious about how others go about it. Sometimes there are good examples, and sometimes there are bad examples. I got to observe both in my family. My siblings are substantially older than me, and so the generational lines are quite blurry in our family. This means that I got to grow up with some of my nieces and nephews and observe my siblings' different approaches to parenting when they had kids of their own. I'm not going to call anyone out directly, lest I stir up some sort of family drama, but let's just say that I gathered a lot of intel that helped shape my own approach to raising kids. The biggest takeaway I gleaned was that parenting is a blessing, and it can be a joy if you choose to see it that way. It can be delightful and worthwhile, unless you see it as a burden—and then it's just duty and work, and often unpleasant. The relationship that you have with your kids is what you make of it. Having some understanding of human development certainly helps with the different challenges that somewhat predictably crop up along the way, but I do believe that attitude is everything here.

And this Mean Dad sitting across from me had a *terrible* attitude toward parenting. Big, humongous turn-off. I drained my wine and hurried our conversation along after that, declining a second glass. When I suggested that we split the bill, he eagerly accepted and then proceeded to do some complicated math (which actually stuck me with most of the bill). Whatever. At that point, I would've happily paid the entire thing to get far away from that guy's energy. That said, I did carry with me some sadness for him and his kids afterward. He was missing out on such a beautiful opportunity to have a meaningful relationship with his children. What a shame. And not a good omen for any of his future romantic relationships, either. If he's that nasty and stingy toward his kid, why would he be any different with a partner? I suspected that he was destined to remain a bitter, lonely, and ultimately unhappy miser. I wanted no part of it, or him. Next!

# Motor Mouth

♥

I t was a cute, kinda teddy-bearish guy who caught my eye next. We met at a waterfront bar for happy hour drinks and snacks. He worked a corporate job in sales and was funny with a quick wit. He had me, the waitress, and the people at surrounding tables in fits of giggles. He was also a very fast talker and expected me to keep up. I didn't even try! I prefer to be thoughtful and take my time to savor questions before forming an answer—it's just who I am. This obviously annoyed him a little but, being tough, I held my ground.

In the past, I likely would've been intimidated by his ability to think and speak so fast and by his expectation that I do the same. But I've grown since then, and I understand myself better these days. In fact, if I could've thought fast enough on that date, I would've spewed out this pointed quote by Canadian/American commentator David Brooks: *"If we are going to accompany someone well, we need to abandon the effi-*

*ciency mind-set. We need to take our time and simply delight in another person's way of being."* Beautifully said.

Before I found books that changed my life (like *Quiet* by Susan Cain and *The Introvert's Way* by Sophia Dambling), I was an apologetic introvert. I grew up in a family, in a generation, and in a culture that *highly* values extroversion—a way of being in the world that demands lots of "peopling" and talking but not a lot of downtime. Essentially, what some might call being "outgoing" or a "go-getter." The conventional wisdom is that embracing and cultivating these traits is the path to success in this world.

I don't jive with that brand of wisdom. My temperament has always been more on the reserved side, and I usually feel better observing than being center stage. That doesn't mean that I never pipe up, but I'm careful and judicious with the words I speak. I have a little ham in me that comes out under certain conditions, but I don't think I've ever been accused of being overly chatty. However, in small groups with the right people, I like talking. I don't ever really enjoy small talk (why on earth do people feel the need for inane chitchat while waiting in line?), though I can do it if the situation requires it. But it just feels pointless and boring. I'd rather talk about real, more meaningful stuff. That might make me sound like a stiff, but let me just clarify by saying that in my mind, "meaningful" conversations can include discussions of the works of Simone de Beauvoir right alongside Mike

Meyers' treasure trove of silly movies, how best to boil beans and the merits of A Flock of Seagulls in the context of '80s music. It doesn't always have to be a serious subject to be interesting to me, but sometimes it is.

That sparkly kind of person who commands the room when they enter, remembers everybody's name, and collects a horde of new friends wherever they go? Yeah, that's not me. The idea that I'd have to learn and perhaps force myself to be that way if I wanted to be successful in life was incredibly discouraging and anxiety-provoking to me as a young person. I felt weak for not being motivated enough to change and shoehorn myself into this kind of personality. And that made me feel not good enough, in general. Nevertheless, I resigned myself to stretching and contorting myself into compliance with varying levels of success over the years. It was exhausting.

But after my dad and brother died, I stopped trying. Partly because I no longer had my dad to please in this way and partly because I just didn't give a fuck anymore. Changing my personality began to seem pointless. I gave up.

And thank god I did, because now I understand that my introverted personality is actually a superpower! I'm not made *wrong*, I'm just made *different*. More importantly, I have a lot to contribute to the world *because* of how I am, not *despite* it. That was a huge paradigm shift I gained from discovering those books and reading more about introversion and extroversion. So this was hard-won progress that I wasn't about to let Motor Mouth undo.

We booked a second date. I'm not entirely sure why I said yes—maybe because I felt that I had something to prove on this score. Not the healthiest response to being challenged, but all I can say is that my confidence in this area was new. Our second meetup went much like the first, and before long, Motor Mouth was flipping me shit for taking too long to answer. I shot back with something about how he could either have a good answer or a fast answer, but not both. That kind of shut him up a little, after which we laughed about it and proceeded to actually have a fun date. I felt strong standing up for myself and, feeling emboldened, I said yes to a third date. This sparring was turning into a bit of fun!

But the third date never happened, and this is why: he invited me to his place for dinner. Nothing wrong with that in theory, but he lived out in the boondocks and I wasn't ready to be alone with him and have no cell reception. No way was I going to risk it after just two dates with a man who was basically still a stranger that I met on the internet. I was honest but kind about the reason for my refusal, but he took it personally and we never spoke again. Why do men have such a hard time understanding women's fears in this regard? Sadly, violence against women by men is common, and we need to be careful and not put ourselves in vulnerable positions—I don't care how "nice" somebody seems. I wish that Motor Mouth would've been more understanding about this, but he wasn't, and so I motored on.

# Rude Dude

♥

Searching for prospects online one day, I was stopped by a profile featuring lots of dark hair and intense eyes. Digging a bit deeper, he seemed like he could be a good possibility. He was attractive physically of course, but we also had a unique connection—we'd actually attended the same college during a similar timeframe. That could be something fun to talk about. He had a career doing research about nutrition and athletic performance—he seemed dedicated to his work and the topic was interesting to me. And so based on that quick, cursory look through his profile, I decided to chat him up.

If it hasn't been made clear yet, I often have a tendency to overthink and overanalyze things. However, dating profiles are the exception. When I was actively dating, I figured that as long as there were a few appealing points, a physical attraction (based on nothing more than pictures initially, which is imperfect but better than nothing), and no obvious red flags (I'm amazed at the kind of crazy shit people include in their profiles), then I initiated a conversation. If the guy was interested and didn't disqualify himself with virtual chat, then I'd (swiftly) move on to asking for an in-person date. No time for bullshit like waiting around to be asked or otherwise beating around the bush. If he seemed like a reasonable candidate, my goal was to move the conversation to a live gig as soon as possible.

Why the hurry? Well, there were a couple of considerations here. Namely, to rule out the possibility that he'd horribly misrepresented himself in some way, or maybe doesn't actually even really exist (it happens). It's also easy to get sucked in to a virtual relationship and start falling for someone sight unseen (been there!). This is a huge potential pitfall, because until you meet in person, you don't really know if you feel that all-important spark. What if they have great photos, are charming, and are a brilliant conversationalist, but in person, you discover that they smell bad or are rude to waiters? Or some other turn-off? Or just a plain lack of a turn-*on*? No chemistry? How much time will you have you sunk into this prospect, and all for naught? Meet as soon as possible, what have you got to lose?

I had *nothing* to lose—except perhaps a bit of time—and so I messaged the guy who'd later become known as Rude Dude. He earned that name because before we could even go out on a date, he managed to take himself out of the running.

My usual go-to for making first contact on the dating apps was some pithy little statement or question. Keep it short and sweet, and see if he takes the bait. With him, I made some comment about the university we'd both attended, and what a funny coincidence! He took the bait all right, but what an absolute dick he was about it. He made some comment about us sharing a school wasn't in fact very interesting and was actually quite common in his experience. A surprising response. It's not like the college was in the same city we were currently living in—or even the same state for that matter—but okay, buddy. I tried again to keep the conversation rolling by asking him some things about his research. He wrote back a dry-as-sawdust reply that could've come straight out of an academic paper. He also, not very subtly, implied that I might not understand it. I started to wonder if he only had one speed—asshole mode. Curious and intrigued by his behavior more than anything, I tried again by commenting about something in his response and tried to bring the conversation down to a more personal level. I offered my own love of kale salads (sounds weird to write that, but it's true and it fit the context), and he proceeded to completely shoot me down by explaining that humans can't actually digest raw kale very well, something about the fact that we're missing some enzymes or some other shit like that. *Enough.* He seemed wholly unable—or unwilling—to meet me anywhere in a pleasant conversation universe. He had bad energy basically from the start. Just a jerk or maybe he didn't like me and didn't know how to say. Or perhaps he was just socially awkward—and, granted, text can be weird—but I wasn't about to stick around and find out. Maybe there was potential there if I'd given it more time, but I wanted a partner, not a project. Be off with you, Rude Dude.

# Sexy Bald Guy #3

♥

I was really taking to heart the idea that dating is an opportunity to meet people outside of my usual parameters when I agreed to go out with sexy Bald Guy #3. Yes, another one. What is it with me and the bald guys? You'd think that I've got something against hair. (I don't.)

He couldn't have been further from my usual type: ex-military and a republican. But also smart and handsome, and I'm a sucker for both of those things. What the hell. I went for it without high hopes about how his obvious conservatism might jibe with my bleeding-heart liberalism. Could be fun fireworks!

We met at the local dive bar, since we lived in the same town (cheers to close proximity—a first on my dating journey!). The place is a little rough around the edges, but I've always loved it. We bellied up to the bar and ordered some suds. There was pointed and prickly banter from the get-go about the political divide between us. It didn't feel hateful or disrespectful though; it was more of a teasing, jousting vibe.

He did have a little bit of a tightly coiled, barely restrained energy that was oddly attractive. There's something about a physically strong and masculine man that's appealing, at least on the surface. Talk turned to work, and he vaguely described his position doing something that required a lot of travel. Part of me began to wonder if he was some kind of government agent—a spy or mercenary? (Maybe I'd been reading too many novels of that genre.) But it did feel like there was something mysterious about him; I can't quite explain it, but it was intriguing. Perhaps a touch of leading man or hero energy?

I allowed drinks to lead to dinner, which was a first for me, as I usually do just one drink and done on first dates. Maybe I was waiting to see if he ordered his martinis shaken not stirred, or otherwise revealed his secret identity. He was also just interesting to be around! He had such a different take on things and I was enjoying spending time with him. He was from Chicago (or maybe that was part of his cover story to obscure his real identity?), which is a city I've always wanted to visit. He clearly had a lot of love for his hometown, and he regaled me with all sorts of stories and travel tips and must-eat foods. He was obviously a food lover, so we had that in common.

It was an easy yes to a second date, even though I didn't think that there was a bright future for us in any kind of enduring relationship. I've known couples with differing political beliefs, but I just can't see how that would work. For me, politics comes down to value systems, and I want to match with my man on that. But Sexy Bald Guy #3 was *sexy*, and we were having fun together so I decided not to overthink it and just enjoy his company. Maybe we could be friends (with or without benefits).

Our next date was for a summer wine festival, but I woke up with a splitting headache that day. I'm not usually a headachy type of person, but this was a whopper. I texted him that I didn't think I could make it, and he seemed understanding about it. But I think he took it as a brush off, which wasn't the case at all. He became distant and we never went on another date. Maybe he just changed his mind about me. Or maybe he had to secretly infiltrate some foreign government and stealthily take out a horrible dictator. Or maybe I need to lay off the spy novels. I wasn't totally crushed that we didn't continue since there didn't seem to be a future for us, but I was getting a little tired out by the churn and burn of dating.

# Mr. Right Now

♥

I was a bit sad that Sexy Bald Guy #3 didn't last longer. He could have been a good candidate for Mr. Right Now.

And perhaps it is time to say a little more about what I mean by that term: Mr. Right Now is someone who's game for a period of light commitment—a temporary but mutually agreeable relationship. This type of arrangement might be referred to by other euphemisms, but I prefer Mr. Right Now. He's not Mr. Right and you know it, but he can provide some pleasant companionship along the way. A rest stop, so to speak, on a long and arduous dating journey.

Some might protest that this seems like a waste of time at best and perhaps selfish, even unprincipled at worst. Maybe so, but I think that it depends on your perspective. I do believe that great care must be taken to ensure that both parties desire this type of no-commitment commitment—otherwise, feelings certainly could get hurt on one or both sides. Upfront honesty about your intentions is the best policy here to ensure that neither of you is looking for a long-term relationship with the other. If stronger feelings were to develop over time, it's important to bring that to light right away and address it. I think the kids today call this "catching feelings," and it's a death knell for this type of casual relationship.

As for whether it's a waste of time—again, maybe. If you're looking for Mr. Right, why settle down with Mr. Right Now instead of continuing the search? Personally, I found going out on a lot of dates somewhat taxing (as you've likely gathered by now). As an introvert, I do need time to recharge after socializing, even if I'm having fun. But the energy required to keep scrolling profiles, being charming in chats, and going out night after night and meeting so many new people took a toll. I was committed to getting it right and wouldn't settle for less than Mr. Right, but the dating road was long, demanding, and sometimes lonely. At that point in my quest, I knew that I was making progress, as evidenced by an increasing number of second dates. This confirmed that my methods were working and that the quality of dates were improving. At the same time, I also recognized that I was tired and needed another break so that I could keep going and finish strong. If I wasn't careful, dating burnout could've set in and led to an ill-advised pairing with an unsuitable partner out of loneliness and fatigue.

And here's where things get weird.

Sexy Bald Guy #2, my very first "Mr. Right Now" from earlier in the year, decided to walk back into my life. Yeah, that guy—the one who'd lied about his age for *months*. He contacted me out of the blue after nearly a year had passed and asked for an opportunity to apologize in person. I thought about continuing to ghost him, but since I was still feeling a bit sheepish about that behavior, this seemed like a good opportunity to make things right on my part as well. Maybe we could even be friends; after all, he *was* fun to be around.

I hadn't planned to reinstate him as Mr. Right Now, but it was unavoidable. Our first meeting after the big silence was for a walk on a waterfront trail. After what seemed like a heartfelt apology and some initially stilted conversation, it soon became obvious that there was way too much heat between us to just be friends. I leaned into it. He might have lied to me in the past, but I didn't want to marry him anyway, so who cares? Apparently, not me!

So we put everything behind us and moved ahead with our reignited little romance. And we did it up, too! We went out to nice dinners a couple of times per week and saw Tony Bennett in concert and drank cocktails afterward in a 1950s tribute lounge. We took long drives with the top down and ate at greasy diners. We even took a weekend trip to San Diego, walked on the beach, got sunburned, and drank piña coladas in the pool. We did low-key, cozy things too, like sitting on the front porch while he smoked cigars, cooking at home, and sprawling on the couch to watch Dr. Zhivago on a snowy Saturday afternoon.

It was fun. But slowly, I got that strange feeling again, like I was missing something with him. He had said that he was divorced, but I began to wonder. There were little hints that he might still be married—twirling a non-existent ring on his wedding finger, making up excuses as to why we couldn't meet at his place, and so on. Enter my savior again: St. Google. It didn't take long to track down his wife on social media. I guess they *could* have been separated, but they clearly weren't divorced! They still appeared to be very much married from the looks of her recent posts. Really?

Feeling like the world's biggest idiot, I confronted him, and that's when he ghosted me. How poetic! I couldn't have devised a more appropriate ending to our dalliance. You lie to me, I ghost you, we make up, you lie to me again, and then you ghost *me*. Perfect! What a modern romance. I guess the message here is this: if they lie about one thing, they may lie about something else. Or maybe even everything!

Perhaps I'm too naïve—maybe more people lie like this than I want to accept. But I refuse to become jaded and assume the worst about people. Okay, I believed your lies, buddy—but there's no shame in that for me. *You* are the one who's fucked up and can't be truthful. That's your integrity on the line, not mine.

I believe that most people are good, and if that means that I get sucked in once in a while, well, so be it. I'll take my chances. But I'll also go Reagan on you: I'll damn well "trust but verify" on stuff that pricks my bullshit detector. And despite these two examples with this one guy, I usually have very good people sense. But, clearly, that sense is never infallible. Let my mistake be your reminder!

# The Dancin' Dad

♥

A sweet, nerdy engineer 10 years my senior who loved to dance contacted me after that previous snake in the grass slithered away. I was left feeling like a chump from that encounter, so this safe guy was the perfect antidote. I'm not a dancer myself, but I like it when people have strong passions—it just seems to make them more interesting. I've never felt like much of a joiner either, but this guy was *so* committed to his swing dancing club. As in multiple times per week spent dancing the night away.

After we finally met in person, it seemed even more interesting to me how such an apparently shy guy could be a demon on the dance floor. Go figure. We went on several dates—none of them dancing—and they were nice. He was a divorced dad of a young son, a good conversationalist and willing and able to talk intelligently about all variety of things. We went out to eat, for walks, some wine tasting and

I found him to be invariably calm, gentle and objectively very handsome. So what was the problem?

On paper? Nothing at all—he was perfect. But in person? Not one iota of chemistry. Sure, he had some quirks that I didn't care for much, like swishing water from his glass to rinse his teeth at the table after dinner, but I'm sure that wouldn't have been a deal breaker. Plus, good dental hygiene is commendable. And I didn't agree with him posting pics of his kid (who was under 10 at the time) on social media. I know he was proud of the kid's dancing competition wins, but I feel strongly that minor children should be kept off our feeds. Once they're adults (or close enough to it) and can consent, fine—fair game. Again, this could've been a conversation, not a reason for rejection. But you know something? I just didn't care enough to keep moving forward with him.

He checked a lot of boxes on my list—kind, intelligent, motivated, engaged with life, a good dad, physically attractive, a deep thinker, and he liked to go out and do fun things. I also appreciated that he had passions and interests of his own. I definitely don't want to date a clone of myself. I think the best relationships are when you align in the ways that matter but have differences that keep things interesting. I also like time by myself, and so any partner I'd be with long term would need to be able to entertain themselves on their own a fair amount. I don't do clingy.

Even though there's some naughty saying about good dancers making good lovers, I had no desire to find out if that held true in this case. He just didn't spark any desire within me. I probably could've had a pleasant, safe, enjoyable relationship with him, but my heart wanted more than that. Passion and excitement were important parts of the dream. The true love story. And I wanted it all.

After serving time in the dating trenches, it could've been easy to give in to the siren call of coupledom—to just find a solid partner, settle down, and move on already, to stop being so picky. But I took strength from the promise I'd made to myself from the outset: I wasn't going to settle for less than perfect. (Remember—perfect for *me*, not perfect in an objective way because that doesn't exist and would probably be boring.) But I wanted the whole package, and that included a man with a package I wanted. Is that too naughty to say? I don't think so. Anyhow, it's true!

I'd come so far, I couldn't give up now—that would be such a cop out. So I sent the Dancin' Dad back to the dance floor and picked up my place in dating land. I was surely weary, but most definitely wiser this time.

# Doomed Darren

♥

By this point, I was feeling more than just a little bit battle scarred, discouraged, and jaded. With all that joyous energy, I managed to attract Darren, a recently retired mailman. Coincidence? Certainly not!

That said, Darren was a hoot! With a sense of humor as dry as I like my martinis, funky eyeglasses, a bit of a paunch, and a touch of alcoholism to boot, I was smitten. He was just such a lively character, almost like he'd stepped out of a sitcom. His stories about the inner workings—or maybe bumblings—at the postal service were hilarious. Seriously, he should've been writing all that shit down to share with generations to come. I hadn't laughed or smiled that much in weeks—maybe months or even years.

We hit it off over drinks (my one to his several), traded war stories from the dating front, and compared divorce histories (his marriage had been 10 years long, no kids). He teased me to no end about my strict dating policies and stinginess with second dates, and I teased right back that I'd go on a second date with him, so my standards must not be that high. We just played off one another, and I felt like I'd known him forever. Not sure if there was a spark—maybe a little brotherly vibe, actually—but there was definitely a lot of fun.

He didn't take me up on my offer for a second date, and I was a little sad about it. I love to laugh like that; it's just so therapeutic. So after a couple of weeks passed, I called him again and got a little pushy. *C'mon, man—we had fun together! Let's hang out, even if only as friends.* The day I called him happened to be his birthday, and he was celebrating with family during the day, but he agreed to meet up in the late afternoon for a summer swim in the river with me.

By the time I arrived after work at around 5, he was well-lubricated with booze from out of his loaded cooler. Barely able to hold a conversation, we still managed to have some laughs, splashed about in the water, and baked in the sun. I offered to drive him home, but he said that he had a ride. I cajoled him into agreeing to get together again in the future—no romance or dates, just fun and companionship. Something we both agreed that we needed. I went home happy with cheeks tired from smiling and laughing so much.

But then Darren went dark. No calls or texts. Fuck—ghosted again! I called and left a joking voicemail taunting him a little with good humor.

A week or so later, I saw that I had a missed call from Darren's number. And a voicemail, but not from him—from a family member informing me that Darren had taken his own life, the day after his birthday.

Stunned and sobered. That's how I felt.

How could he just end himself like that? In his 50s and newly retired, he'd reached a level of freedom that most of us spend decades of our lives working toward—waiting for the fun part of life to begin when we have fewer responsibilities, no 9-to-5 jobs or awful bosses. And when we qualify for cheap health insurance. Life was just about to get good! But I guess Darren did his brand of math differently.

I'd be lying if I said I've never contemplated suicide myself. I've had my dark days, especially during the treat that's the menopause transition (that'll be another book I write—no lie), but never seriously considered it a real option. But I also have a lot keeping me here, especially my kids. And I'm grateful that I've stuck around, because it *is* true what they say—it *does* get better.

I wish that Darren had stuck around just a little while longer so that he could've found this out for himself.

# Mr. Right Now #2

♥

Even more weary and disillusioned about dating after Darren's suicide, I took a big break from shopping for mates online. I went into passive mode. I just didn't have the heart for sifting through profiles, winking, and chatting. I started to wonder: *Maybe I'm just not meant to have true love in this lifetime?*

And right then, Mr. Right Now #2 slid into my DMs (that's "direct messages" for the older crowd).

He made a joke about the small town I was living in being a dustbowl for dateable men, and suggested that I let him console me about that. I laughed out loud—it was true. Though my neighborhood might be safe, pretty, and have excellent schools, it was mostly families that lived there raising kids. Not exactly a hotspot for finding single men. The confident banter perked me up a bit, and so I decided to take him up on the offer for a date.

Stepping outside of my usual dating parameters, I traveled to meet him at his favorite brewery in his neighborhood. It was a cute community with an average brewpub (they're a dime a dozen in these parts), situated near a college. He was a handsome and gregarious guy, but not even halfway through my first beer, he was detailing his polyamorous lifestyle.

Sweet Jesus! At least let me get through my pilsner without spewing suds out my nose. I don't usually consider myself a conservative person—in fact, I find myself most often on the side of questioning authority and everything else—but polyamory? Isn't that just a convenient way to label and justify being unable or unwilling to commit to one partner?

My moral compass momentarily twanged (it's how I was raised) but curiosity piqued, I asked him to tell me more.

He started to recount his experiences with monogamy and marriage, both disappointing. He'd had a couple of post-divorce, unsatisfying relationships and was abruptly facing his own mortality since a close friend of his had died unexpectedly. In radical life-affirming mode, he discovered the polyamorous lifestyle, in which multiple people commit to each other (it's not just swingers). Sometimes they live together, but not always. Sometimes they marry, but not always. Imagine if Jack was openly dating both Chrissy and Janet on Three's Company—that would be an example of polyamory (as I understand it, anyway; I'm not really an expert). But the way this guy was telling it, he wasn't sure how much time he'd have left on Earth and wanted to go out and get as much lovin' as he possibly could before his number came up. Best way to do that? Have multiple partners, apparently. Still feels like a way to sleep around with permission, but I try not to judge (too harshly).

As he was relatively new to the lifestyle, he only had one partner but was looking to add a second (guess who? Me!). His arguments for the merits of polyamory were interesting, if not completely convincing. Although it did sound nice to have companionship and sex on speed dial without a lot of messy commitment, I wasn't even vaguely interested in having multiple partners—or in getting to know Mr. Right Now #2's other lady, which I guess is the norm in that world. Being friends with some random woman, even though we're sleeping with the same guy (but not each other, just to be clear)? No thanks on that. Not for me.

We finished our beers and he walked me up the street to my car with my head spinning from his unexpected admission. His eyes twinkled at me as he told me I was pretty and that he wanted to spend more time with me. A lovely kiss followed, and I drove home, admittedly thinking about the possibilities.

I did like him. Even though I knew this wasn't the type of arrangement I'd want long term, maybe it would be okay as a gap filler. And I certainly had zero interest in juggling multiple men myself or meeting his other ladies, but if he wanted to see other women at the same time as me, go for it I guess. As an introvert, I kind of liked the idea of having company when I wanted it, as well as plenty of time by myself. To be honest, it sounded good not being the only person available should my partner desire company when I was craving solitude.

So what the hell—I decided to go for it. It'd be interesting (if nothing else).

All appropriate measures to ensure safe sex between the three of us were obviously taken, and so thus commenced my second Mr. Right Now relationship. During our time together, we went out for more beers, watched movies at his place, he cooked me dinner a couple of times, and even brought me breakfast in bed. He seemed to like to pamper me and, I confess, I enjoyed the hell out of that. He was smart, could hold up his end of a good conversation, wasn't afraid of showing his emotions, and went out of his way to make me feel like a treasured person. It was fun and light—and lasted all of four or five dates. I tried my best to just sink into the moment and enjoy (sharing) Mr. Right Now #2, but it was no use. Having some parts of a "real" relationship made me want *all* the parts even more. I explained to him that I thought he was great but that I wanted the traditional love story—the one with two people loving each other through the end of time, not three or four or five of us. That seemed too crowded for my taste. I decided that I'd rather have no relationship than a partial one. No relationship timeshares for me. He was gracious and understanding and said that he'd leave the door open for me in case I ever changed my mind.

I didn't. Who knows how many other liberal lovers ended up walking through his revolving door and sharing his time? It just wasn't the door for me.

# Resignation

♥

I fished around for dates halfheartedly for a little while longer, but I just wasn't into it anymore. Instead of persisting or taking another break from dating, I went into full-on hermit mode. Honestly, giving up on love and entering a convent did cross my mind. Since I'm not the least bit religious, that was not a viable option.

Resignation is a bit of a sad word, but I honestly didn't feel sad when I decided to give up on dating and finding true love. Maybe searching for Mr. Right was a dead end and, ultimately, unnecessary. I think many of us have lost the talent for being alone. But we can grow that muscle again and even (gasp!) dare to enjoy our own company.

By all accounts, my life was pretty damn good. As previously mentioned, I had healthy and happy kids, a nice house, a good job, and friends and family to support me and have fun with. I also had my pick of Mr. Right Nows if I ever desired companionship in the future. And I liked myself and my life just fine as it was. For me, solitude was something to enjoy—not dread as it is for so many others. I felt centered, loved, and basically happy. I finally understood that a relationship was not vital to my existence. They aren't oxygen. I could live without one. Love would be an extra bonus, but far from required for my wellbeing. And that's an amazing place to be in life, so let's just take a moment to appreciate that.

I clearly remember talking with my dear friend on the phone about this epiphany of mine. She's always a reliable person for going into deep conversation mode at a moment's notice, and she immediately met me where I was. She asked a lot of astute questions, closely listened to my answers, and validated all my feelings. She didn't even once try to talk me out of my move to embrace a solo life. In fact, being a twice-married person herself, she offered that, in many ways, staying single has a lot going for it. Freedom, independence, room for a dog in the bed. Less emotionally messy, for sure. Life can still be great—even single.

I hung up from our call feeling seen and understood. Not like a failure or a defeatist, but as someone who knows her own mind and had made a logical, well-reasoned choice for herself. I might be alone, but I was happy, not lonely and would still have a good life.

And that's exactly when the love of my life entered the picture. The universe can be crazy that way.

# *Mr. Right*

♥

*"The three biggest green flags are growth, kindness, and compassion.*
*If they are consistently kind, if they care about growing, and if they*
*can see beyond their own perspective, then this is someone worth*
*your time and energy."*

—Yung Pueblo, American author

As mentioned, I was in the "happily enough" throes of resignation, and so I went back to the dating site to shut down my profile. Lo and behold—a reply to a message I'd sent quite a while before to a smiley, dark-haired man—Steven. I really *was* done dating and looking for love, but it seemed imprudent to just ignore his message. I mean, I may be a lot of things, but I'm not rude! Plus, I was super curious. But my oh my—how quickly that resolve to embrace singledom crumbled!

It had been a while since I'd sent him the note and, trying to remember what had initially attracted me to this guy, I hightailed it back over to his profile. Big, genuine smile. Lots of pictures of him doing creative and fun things. A thoughtful personal statement and engaged in very interesting creative work that he seemed passionate about. Okay, it was very easy to see why I'd been interested in him!

I don't remember now what his first message to me said (*he* probably does, as he's got a memory like a steel trap), but I do remember how it made me feel: excited. Maybe there was hope for love yet! Again, it seemed silly not to at least get to know the guy, even if there was little hope by this point. So I did just that.

Fun banter ensued virtually, but we were both intent on meeting in person, and soon. He offered the choice of either a (snooty) wine place or a (fun!) dive bar. I immediately picked the dive bar, and he seemed delighted by my choice. If it was a test, I'd apparently passed. Not that I was even trying to pick the "right" thing—I just chose what honestly sounded best to me. Dive bars feel more down to Earth and gritty, where the people are real. I love wine too, don't get me wrong—I'm a winemaker's daughter after all. But dive bars are just silly fun and *way* more relaxed for a first date. So even though this was off playbook and not at my usual first date joint, I delightedly went along with it.

Since we were breaking the rules, I picked a different outfit to wear, too. A bright yellow dress instead of my usual green one. And boots instead of sandals because I was feeling kind of badass. It was time for a fresh start.

I may have a propensity for bald guys—three of them right here in this book, and that's not even all of them—but let me tell you: my true love has a full head of dark hair (and even more on his chest, but I didn't find that out until later. Meow!). I spotted him and that gorgeous hair walking into the bar from a safe distance due to my intentionally late entrance.

We had our first contact at the bar where he was standing in line to order. He smelled good and looked even better. A kind face and an infectious smile. But what really drew me in were his eyes—deep, and wise like he's seen something of life and not all of it good. A man who has been tested by life and survived. Swoon!

Some fun coincidences abounded during the course of our conversation, and actually some not-so-fun ones, too. A brilliant, no-holds-barred, antithesis-to-small-talk kind of conversation. Absolute heaven! We learned that we both love martinis and books, having read many of the same authors. We also discovered a shared love of food, family, and travel. In the not-so-fun column, we'd both suffered through painful divorces and had lost close family members in recent years.

It's odd to admit that we bonded over our shared grief and actually cried together on our first date, but it's true. There was a weird, kind of mystical connection between us from the get-go, and we both felt it. It might sound cliche, but I felt like I'd known him all my life—like something in me recognized something in *him*. I won't get too wacky on this here, but it did feel supernatural somehow. Maybe I'll just sum up the feeling we both had with one on my favorite quotes by American author bell hooks: *"When we love, we can let our hearts speak."* I don't think I'd ever felt this sentiment more than on that first meeting. My heart felt completely open to this man I had just met.

The date was over three-hours long but felt like the blink of an eye. Steven walked me to my car and we were already planning our next date, for soon. We hugged—no kiss yet—and I drove home feeling a heady mix of excitement, peace, and calm. As well as a surreal combination of certainty and confidence, or something like that. He, sort of sheepishly, called me soon after I got home on that same night. As humans who perform this dating dance, we're all brainwashed not to seem too eager, and that's such bullshit. But he just wanted to see how I felt about our date from a distance. Had I changed my mind on the drive home? Hell, no! Was I still interested in a second date? Hell, yes! I couldn't *wait* to see him again. I went to sleep with a giddy smile plastered on my face. I felt like a goon—a lovestruck goon.

Our second date occurred just two days later. We met for lunch at a cute, outdoor pizza joint. The conversation continued to flow from one open heart to the other. The discovery period of a new and exciting relationship is so much fun! After wine and pizza, we shared our first kiss in the parking lot and never looked back. It was a solid *yes* to each other from that moment forward.

Our first "I love yous" happened a month later in a dive bar. Thirteen months after that, Steven enlisted the kids to ask me to marry him. I can honestly say that our first year was the happiest time in my life. Don't get me wrong—we are still deliriously happy together now!—but that year of so many wonderful firsts was such a contrast to the shitty years of deaths and divorce that it shone extra brilliantly and blindingly. I kept feeling like I needed to shake myself awake. How could *I* be the center of a real-life love story? But I was.

How did I know that Steven was "the one?" I say that with tongue firmly in cheek because the concept of there only being one right person out there for each of us is utter hogwash! The numbers just don't add up, but I digress, back to how I knew Steven was right for me: I expected that I'd conduct a rational review of his credentials to be my leading man and a clear-eyed comparison of the pros versus cons of making the relationship permanent, followed by a reasoned decision. Ha! Listen, not that some of those computations weren't going on in the back of my mind, but it was really all gut. I generally loathe when people give answers like this, but I just knew at a soul level that he was my guy. Unlike in other relationships in which there was compromise and accepting *this* about him because I liked *that* part of him, a resounding *yes* echoed through my heart and mind. And it wasn't just the lovestruck phase at the beginning of a new relationship either. This was the real deal.

Upon reflection though, he'd nailed almost every single one of the items I had on my list of desired traits. (If you're curious, you can check out my actual list at the end of the book, because it really did exist.) Every single one of the most important things, he had on lock. Plus, some things I hadn't thought to include, but he brought them to the table anyway—like his calm, thoughtful approach to making inroads with my kids. Of course, when I was thinking about finding love I wanted someone who'd get along with my kids, although I hadn't considered the details of how that might happen. But *he* had.

An even deeper read revealed a fascinating fact: Steven is an amalgamation of all the desirable traits I liked in various men from my past, but present *all* in the same person. A few things I love and appreciate about him are that he's smart, fun and funny, burly and masculine, dark-haired and kind, motivated, talented, highly emotionally intelligent, introspective, curious, creative, and good in bed. I also love how I feel when I'm with him—like my best self. I've always craved feeling understood like I am now on a deep, soul level, and I think that we all do. In addition, he is a master listener and encourager. I could go on, but I'm trying to resist turning this book into a love letter to my husband! However, I am a lucky, lucky woman to have met and fallen in love with this man. He is truly a rare gem. And he thinks that I'm pretty great, too.

Our first wedding (we had two!) was magical and absolutely on par with our love story. I'd suggested a time and place that had significance in my family—the same day of the year and location where my parents eloped as crazy, 17-year-old kids. Their marriage endured for 57 years before my dad died. Their union was always celebrated in our family and held up as a good example worth emulating. I do think that they're a solid illustration of how you can commit to a person, remain loyal, and stay the course. Were they deliriously in love? Were they truly a good fit? To be honest, I'm not entirely sure, but they *did* go the distance. And they successfully raised six kids together and made it through their share of hardships. I know that they found each other attractive, and sometimes I observed this in highly embarrassing ways (trust me—you don't want *those* details). Were they deeply connected at a soul level? Maybe not, but they were from a different generation that I believe was more practical about marriage.

They were very different people in many ways. My dad was a consummate extrovert who traveled a lot for work, loved meeting new people, and was a lifelong learner and deep thinker. My mom is an introvert, loves maintaining pretty homes, is a super athlete, and takes care of business without a lot of sentimentality or fuss. When I was growing up at home, there was always an undercurrent of obstinance between them, like they were both fighting against each other to be understood and accepted and, perhaps, right. It was sort of painful for me to witness that as a kid, because I got the message that I should try to keep them both happy and getting along. But I guess it worked well enough for them to stay together.

Even though the lore that had built up around mom and dad's marriage had lost some of its luster to my adult eyes, I still liked the idea of following their example for our first wedding. I am a sentimental romantic, and so we eloped—just like they did on the same date 63 years later. Just the two of us, three friends to witness, and one to marry us—in the middle of an honest-to-goodness blizzard. Still, it was the most romantic day of my life. I hate pictures of myself (you'll recall my photo phobia mentioned previously), but I love the ones of me from this day. You can see the genuine joy on my face that reaches my eyes (check out the author picture for the evidence of this!).

Our second wedding was a more traditional affair in the summer to celebrate with our family and close friends. Dress, tux, hair, make-up, our kids as attendants, and a big, boozy dinner in a wine cave with a well-curated playlist (naturally, since we both love music). Lots of merriment followed by a madcap dive-bar trip in our wedding clothes, where the whole place was congratulating us and buying rounds of drinks. Both events were fun and meaningful ways to mark our commitment to each other. Treasured memories. I'm smiling to myself right here and now as I write to you about our fantastic launch into married life.

*Obviously*, we lived happily ever after.

# 7 Years Later: Happily Married to Mr. Right

♥

**W**ell, not so fast.

A relationship is never a fairytale, no matter how good of a fit you are together. I've definitely come to realize that a good fit is essential to successful coupledom, but it isn't the only thing. You can't just go out there and find a suitable person and never make any effort again. The cool part though, is that when you fit together well, the effort feels *easy*. When your temperaments, values, generational experience, and natural inclinations all sync up, it's a magical feeling.

When Steven and I first got together, we were so clearly and sickeningly in love that my brother said we were in the honeymoon phase and that effect would surely wear off. But seven years later, we're still going strong. How? Why? Other than choosing your partner wisely, what's the secret to *staying* in love?

I'll tell you how this works: stay on the same side, as a team, no matter what you are facing and make loving your mate a habit. Those two things. Below, I'll run through some of the challenges we've faced as a couple, followed by some of the ways that we maintain our connection—no matter what life throws at us. Because the path hasn't always been smooth! Remember, fairytales don't exist.

# Shit We Weathered

We have not lacked for difficult circumstances, small and large, to test our resolve to remain together, strong as a team. I remember a few years into our relationship we had a discussion about it.

"So why are *we* ok with *this*?" my husband asked. By "this" he was referring to the dodgy room we were staying in for our lil' romantic (pandemic respectful) getaway. We laughed and contemplated this question while perched gingerly on rickety chairs, drinking the awful, but blessedly alcoholic complimentary wine and willing ourselves to go nose blind to the smell of the place – a musky top note of animal urine with an underlying hint of mold.

He wasn't asking why we were strong (or stupid) enough to endure this, but more what sets us apart from the many other couples we knew who wouldn't be able to get past the immediate awfulness of this situation to find the fun and be *ok* with it.

I think we were ok with this disappointing shit hole for precisely the same reasons we were ok with the pandemic. And raising teenagers. And caring for an elderly parent with declining health. And economic hardships and plumbing disasters and menopause. Because, in challenging situations such as these, we manage to remain united rather than expanding the conflict to include each other. I've been in that other kind of relationship where things went the other way and this kind of wrinkle in the plans would turn into a blame fest (you should have researched this room better! I can't stay here! You've ruined our vacation!). And so has Steven. It also doesn't hurt that we genuinely like each other and are pretty resilient as individuals (hard won through our share of bad experiences).

Ever the optimist, Steven pointed out that we learned some stuff about ourselves in sewer city—that we can have fun anywhere, that we can look for the good in any situation (we did have a stunning sunny walk on the beach prior to checking in) and, we had choices and didn't have to stay in that shitty place. We both agreed we would just pack ourselves up, jump in the car and retreat a day early to our beloved happy home to continue our romantic getaway there. Minus the stench and aggressive black flies. This wasn't the first or last time we were tested! Read on for more.

Family Resistance

When you get into a relationship with someone, their family and loved ones are also part of the deal. And families are far from perfect. Every one has its quirks and when you grow up in one, those quirks seem "normal". Coming in as an outsider it may be shocking to see the norms your partner has acquired and tempting to point them all out! Please resist the urge; family is sacred, even if they seem very fucked up. You can't make fun of it, unless your partner does so first and even then you need to tread lightly.

People make different decisions for themselves about what they are willing to tolerate for the sake of maintaining their family connections. Its an individual thing. You need to allow your partner to decide that for themselves and not judge them for it. Or make ultimatums. This is not an "it's me or them type" of situation. To force this kind of choice is unfair and unloving to your partner who just wants both of you to be happy. It is best if you accept that your partner and their family are a package deal and not expect any of that to change to suit you. Your partner gets to lead on this one.

That being said, don't stay with someone if you really can't stand their family. Especially if your partner thinks they are great and wants to have dinner with them every Sunday night. You might be thinking that you can simply duck out of those events or keep contact to a minimum, but then you would be missing the whole point. Your partner loves both you and their family and wants you to connect on some level. If you can't do that with an open heart and keep your unkind thoughts to yourself about Uncle Joe's shady business deals during family gatherings, then maybe you should rethink the relationship. Particularly if you are already entertaining thoughts about how you wouldn't want children of yours to grow up around those people. Your partner is going to feel that tension no matter how much you try to hide it. Continuing on together when you are poorly matched in this way is serving no one. It is a recipe for ongoing discord and best avoided.

Steven and I definitely had our own challenges to navigate in this area. I've always been tight with my parents and brothers and sisters, but my position as "the baby" of the family comes with persistent aggravations. Even though I was pushing 50 when Steven and I got together, my family still treated me like I was a clueless child in many ways. It's like I grew up and they didn't notice. They have a strong tendency to see what is potentially wrong with a situation and how I am managing it. This pattern led me to feel incredibly discouraged at times, especially when I was in the midst of an epic love story! There were lots of questions about my decision to be with him, to marry (*"Can't you just live together?"*), and heaps of other unsolicited opinions. I know it was all probably coming from a good place, but good god, have a little faith in me already!

I'd managed to navigate life to that point objectively well, despite one divorce. I was healthy, had a solid career, was self-sufficient, and was doing a good job raising my kids. It's not like I was a clueless airy-fairy who didn't know her ass from her elbow! But yet—*sigh*—this family of mine can be clannish and quick to judge, and they just had to insinuate themselves into my decision about who to love. How they could object to Steven (who in my mind is one of the least objectionable people on the planet) is hard for me to understand, but they managed to do it. And they didn't really take it well when I claimed boundaries about this. With time, most of them have eventually come to grudgingly accept that we're a good match and that he's a good man, but it was disillusioning and sobering to go through. Having my family resist something that felt *so* right—righter than anything else in my life—was disheartening.

He was understandably hurt—he cares and is a sensitive man who likes being liked (who doesn't?). But he wisely let me deal with my family shit the way I needed to. He stayed kind and authentic throughout, because that's who he is. However, he did have very strong opinions about how we should best approach the kids.

Even though my man and I were all-in on each other and full speed ahead, we knew that we had to bring our kids along gradually. His kids were both adults, so I had a fairly easy time relating to and being accepted by them. We would get together for dinners and conversation and it was all pretty low-key. However, my kids, being pre-teens and still living at home, were a different story. I knew that I didn't want to drag them into every dating (mis)adventure I had, but if I'm asked for any kind of specific criteria I was applying to the question of when to introduce someone I was dating, I really don't have a straight answer. I guess I'm more of an intuitive person on stuff like that, but I knew that I didn't want them meeting every Tom, Dick, and Sexy Bald Guy. In fact, Steven was the first and only guy I'd dated that they met. Because with him, I was sure. Thankfully, Steven recognized the wisdom in playing the long game with them when we got together. We were extra careful and waited a couple of months before even having the first, low-pressure, face-to-face meeting.

They knew about Steven and that he was special from how I'd talked about him and they were curious, if a little shy and trepidatious. We decided on a brief, casual meet on Halloween. They'd be out running around the neighborhood with their friends and could come by for a glimpse of him while we sat on the front steps doling out candy. It worked great! And it certainly didn't hurt that the dog had immediately accepted him (and that dog hates *everyone*). Amazingly, our furry beast spent the night perched happily in Steven's lap! As our relationship progressed, we eased into doing stuff as a foursome—walks, dinners, and eventually sleepovers and short trips. We didn't live together until we married, and we moved Steven in slowly after tying the knot.

To tell you the truth, he treated them like wild deer visiting the backyard—staying calm and quiet to let them get used to his presence. Admittedly, it was downright painful how slow this process was, but we both knew it was the correct approach. You can't force children to like and accept your new mate. There were a lot of years—yes, *years*—of sullen silence from the kids toward Steven. He was often discouraged because he is a really sweet man, and kids in general tend to love him (just not mine! Not at the time, anyhow). I understood then that it wasn't about Steven—it was about the space he now suddenly occupied in my life—but that didn't make it any easier.

I never second-guessed my love for my husband or getting married again, but I did question the timing after all was said and done. As pre-teens, my kids were developmentally at a very self-involved stage of life that we all go through. And even though I believe that they wanted me to be happy in the abstract, me having an actual, living, and breathing (and staying) man in my life was a bit too real for them. Plus, they were still shellshocked from my divorce and understandably wary of another marriage. I get it! I did then, and I do now. I remember fearing that I'd fucked up by getting married too soon—*"Maybe we should've waited until they were in college or something."* And I also questioned changing my last name to his—the kids felt a little abandoned since we no longer shared the same last name. Oops. But I didn't really want to be Mrs. Who-I-Used-To-Be anymore, since my former husband had remarried and there was someone new using that name. Also, I like the tradition of sharing a last name with my spouse. But maybe I should've given that more time, too. I take my role as mom *very* seriously, and so to feel like I was fucking up left and right was gutting at the time. I feared that my happiness in love was going to cost me the wellbeing of my kids. Turns out that was overblown anxiety running amok on my part, and we all eventually adjusted—but it was a thorny road there for a while.

I must give Steven credit though, because he hung in there. He could've acted hurt or called them out or, worse, asked *me* to call them out on their behavior toward *him*, but he didn't. He's the one who had the insight that there was no good to come of us insisting that my kids be nice and inclusive toward him—it would only further alienate and increase their resentment. I validated his hurt feelings in private, and we soldiered on together. I'm convinced that a weaker man would've folded.

He was always—and continues to be—encouraging of me to do what I feel is best for the kids. He never *ever* made me feel like I needed to choose between him and them. He held me, consoled me, and advised me during difficult parenting challenges, but he also let me lead. He strove for "funny uncle" status, not "stepdad." There were a lot of painfully pun-y jokes and silliness, but also deep conversation and wise counsel as they grew up and began to accept those things from him. Steven stayed steady, knowing that even though they didn't say much, their eyes were *always* watching us. He never lost sight of who he was and stayed authentic, even when met with stony silence and eyerolls. He continued to treat me well, which was never lost on them. Despite the massive cold shoulder and seemingly zero hope, he was always unfailingly kind and considerate toward the kids. Eventually, and amazingly, they finally came around. There were mere glimmers of acceptance at first—accepting rides from him, laughing at his jokes more than just politely—but eventually, their hearts opened.

I remember when my daughter went off to college and got her first taste of homesickness. She asked that we—*we!*—come down for parents' weekend. He was thrilled to be included, and we all had a great time. I think that it took a little distance for her to appreciate what a great guy he is. Now she holds us up as an example of what she wants in a relationship. She even talks about wanting to find her "Steven"!

It was discouraging at times and took ages, but we did navigate those shark-infested waters together and made it to the other shore—family intact. I'm forever grateful that my husband was so wise and considerate about how he approached joining my family. It made all the difference.

Pandemic

Barely a year after we married, the whole world shut down
due to the coronavirus. It was a scary and uncertain time, a
definite test of the strength of our bond in multiple ways.
First, how would we do with so much forced togetherness,
stuck inside with one another for extended periods? Would
the honeymoon effect finally wear off? How would we inter-
pret and respond to the risk of this threat that was developing
and changing right before our eyes? And how would we keep
the kids and ourselves happy and sane?

In short, we did great. Being introverts and basically home-
bodies, the lockdowns and social distancing weren't that difficult for us. And we actually found our bond deepening in the
face of adversity. Instead of turning against each other in this
time of great stress and uncertainty, we turned *toward* each
other. We did our best to make it fun for us, and for the kids
who were less-than-thrilled to be stuck at home with us and
away from their friends. We started having themed dinner
nights—we'd dress up and make food and craft drinks to
match. There was Hawaiian night, Greek night, fancy dinner
night, and steakhouse night—I can't remember everything
else, but it was a pleasure. We also each picked a hobby to
explore. Steven got a bike, my daughter started painting,
and my son and I got guitars and learned to play songs in

our garage. We took the dog for long walks and planted a big garden. There were some major disappointments along the way—the kids being stuck with online school, having to cancel a trip we'd planned to Greece, not being able to see my mom for months—but we made it out the other side. I think our key to survival was that we both went the extra mile to give each other space and grace to not be at our best and to work together to make the best out of a tricky situation. And we succeeded.

Entrepreneurial Endeavors & Career Changes

When I first met Steven, he was an old hand at being self-employed. He already knew what it was like to have the joy of working for yourself and the burden of making a living without having a steady paycheck.

Eventually, I joined him in that. It was an agonizing period of my life, realizing that I'd fallen out of love with my healthcare career. This fraught stage paralleled our relationship timeline. I was starting to have an inkling before we'd even met, but with his guidance and support, I made the difficult decision to face what I didn't want to: my career was making me miserable and I needed to leave it. It was far from an easy transition, but at least I had a wingman to help me through the whole ugly process. I even wrote an entire book about this journey—*Falling Out Of Love with My Career*—and I can confidently say that the story has a happy ending, in more ways than one!

But anyone who's ever worked for themselves knows how stressful it can be. There's the money factor, of course, but also all the other details such as figuring out health insurance and taxes and learning to be okay with a high level of uncertainty. It's incredibly stressful!

It helps that we both have so much gratitude for the life that we now lead—no more bad bosses or punching time clocks or ridiculous commutes. We have the freedom to structure our work lives how we see fit, and it's *glorious!* We both thrive in this type of bohemian, creative lifestyle and have grown to trust that things always work out. Many times one or the other of us will be struggling and the other will step in to provide much needed empathy, guidance and encouragement. I'm so much happier living this life than the other one I had working a regular job. Even with all the extra challenges it brings, it's a delight, and I'm so very grateful that Steven and I get to share this life together.

<u>Perimenopause</u>

He loved me through every hot flash, night sweat, mood swing, and frightful crime scene period. As well as every one of my body sizes, because I did get a little "fluffier" thanks to perimenopause (and the pandemic—let's be honest). He never once made me feel ashamed of myself for having a rough ride at the mercy of my rapidly fluctuating hormones. There were certainly times when I was, admittedly, quite a lot to be around. But he hung in there with me and his steady presence gave me strength to weather all that confusing shit. I'm starting to come out the other side of the process now, but there were some years during which I was incredibly uncomfortable in my body and in my mind, years when I just didn't feel like myself. I made a real effort to communicate all the horrid details and ugly feelings with him (even when I didn't want to), but I knew that I needed to share this journey with him because it was a significant one. Even though I was horrified to be that exposed in front of another person, he made certain I knew that I was loved—no matter what.

Even though I'm sure that it was no fun for him either, he never complained or made me feel bad for how my experience affected him. That was so incredibly gracious of him, and I'm grateful because I had such limited bandwidth. Perimenopause was like a hungry hippopotamus had plunked down in the middle of the room, sucking up almost every ounce of joy in my life. All while I was trying to be a good parent, get a new career off the ground and help out my aging mom. I'm incredibly thankful that I had a true partner to help me make it through and who recognized my "change of life" as just a temporary situation. I hadn't turned into a different person; I was just struggling through a tough time and it would pass, just like a storm blowing through. And it did, with him by my side as every gale and gust threatened us with defeat.

## Conflicting Habits

I'm a minimalist living in Steven's maximalist world.

He collects coffee mugs like we don't have a dishwasher. T-shirts like a washing machine is not a luxury we enjoy. Books like there's no library less than a mile down the road. Sunglasses like he forgets we live in the Pacific Northwest where the sun only shines a few months of the year. And don't even get me started about all the sweets and treats he has squirreled away around the house. He's not at peace unless we have backups of most food items in the pantry for whatever supply chain shortage emergency there may be in the future. I can't even bring myself to discuss the pickle situation.

I, on the other hand, take pleasure in getting rid of stuff. Broken stuff, no-longer-loved clothing even when it is still in good repair, single use gadgets (some of the time) and all manner of clutter are not safe from culling. Thinning out my space is therapeutic for me. I like clean lines and surfaces. It quells my anxiety and makes me feel peaceful. I can breathe easier without a bunch of bric-a-brac around.

It may seem like a minor thing, but we did need to find some sort of agreement on this score or risk being rubbed raw by our differences. So how do we coexist? Mutual respect and effortful understanding.

Looking at his overflowing desk in our shared office sometimes makes me see red, but then I take a deep breath and
remember why he is the way he is. This isn't really my story
to tell, but I do have permission. You see, Steven didn't have
much growing up. He lived a life of true deprivation in a
backwater house with no electricity and subpar parents where
love, security, clothing and even food were scarce. He talks
about these things freely and it breaks my heart every single
time. And that's what I think about when I feel any kind of
resentment rising inside of me about all of his stuff crammed
in to our house and overflowing into a storage unit. It puts it
all back into perspective for me and gives me the patience to
accept that he will feel better about letting things go once he
has experienced enough love, safety and security to fill up that
crater in his child's heart. As someone who loves him deeply,
I want to stay on the right side of that process. That's more
important to me than having things my way, right away. For
his part, he respects my needs too. He makes sure the kitchen
is clean most of the time when I wake up, helps me thin out
the garage abyss at least once yearly and has been forgiving
when I have disposed of stuff willy-nilly and regretted it later.

You see, quirks and habits like these often stem from hurts,
so it is best to be gentle with them. Strive to be helpful, not
dismissive or unkind, as some deep wounds need longer to
heal. In our case, I am confident that with time and patience,
we will find the middle ground that works for both of us, but

for now, we accept the imperfection on both sides and just keep loving each other.

## Homeowner Joys

I mentioned earlier in the book that I've dubbed our house "Haven Home," and here's why it's earned that name: we intentionally developed and maintain a peaceful, creative environment here. Maybe that sounds a little too precious, but we like it. That doesn't mean that Haven Home doesn't have her foibles, though—she's thrown at us sewer backups, burst water pipes, yearly sprinkler troubles, and a mysterious roof leak that took months and tons of money to solve, among many other glitches. Just in the last week alone we had a toilet issue requiring a plumber, the washer died and we had to buy a new one and the garbage disposal became hopelessly blocked with green goo that would not drain (I'm sure that last one was my fault, sorry honey!). Rather than get all upset about these admittedly totally annoying issues, or point fingers, we kept our cool and figured it out.

I can remember one instance when we were guiding a floppy mattress up the stairs, and another time in a paint store picking colors for the exterior of our home when we both just stopped, looked at each other, and thanked the gracious stars above that we could navigate challenges like these peacefully and without conflict. It was a radical departure from past experiences for both of us, experiences where those types of tasks would be filled with relationship landmines. Calm communication and cooperation are our mantras when dealing with this variety of crap.

## Aging Parent

My mom is 86 and on hospice as I write these words. Having worked in end of life care for much of my life, I know this gig well. However, it's decidedly different when it's *your own mom* who you're helping through the dying process. Being the medically trained person amongst my siblings, and the closest to mom geographically, means that the burden of supporting her has fallen on me. I'm totally okay with this, and my siblings do help out when and where they can, but it's a lot. I feel like I'm on-call every hour of every day, and my nervous system is primed to go into action at any moment. It's not good for my anxiety, I can tell you that! But it *is* part of life.

My husband and I have created a fun ritual we call "Martinis with Mom," during which we go over to mom's place, make her a drink and dinner, and have a nice visit. In recent months, our duties have expanded beyond these happy nights to include household chores, shopping, and transportation since she no longer drives. And lots of moral support—to her *and* to each other. It's hard to watch someone you love fading away and getting more debilitated, but we're committed to help her keep living well until she dies. Thank god that Steven sees this as I do—as a worthy endeavor, an act of of love and not just another burden to bear. And that there can still be small joys in the midst of misery.

Travel

Travel is such a great test of the seaworthiness of a relationship. On one hand it's exciting and stimulating to have
shared adventures to new places. On the other, it invariably
involves unexpected challenges and requires extra energy and
concentration to spend time outside of your comfort zone.

I remember when Steven and I took our very first big trip
together after coupling up. Ironically, just like in my first
marriage, we also went to Hawaii. What a difference a mate
makes! We did not have the same challenges as that earlier
trip, where his need for socialization butted up against my
need for time to recharge leaving us both feeling abandoned,
but we still had plenty to tax us.

We arrived in a typhoon which proceeded to flood the local
roads around us, essentially trapping us in our tiny rental spot.
Heavy rains were not part of the picture we had prepared for
our tropical getaway, but we still made it work. We went
to the beach anyway and reveled in the warm showers, so
much different than what we get at home. We drove around
the island and paid our respects at the local dive bars. And
we just rested in each other's company, alone and together.
I was also a bit emotional on the trip due to resurfacing
memories from earlier visits I had made to the area with
my late brother. Steven understood my grief and treated me
kindly and tenderly. So even though it wasn't exactly what

we had in mind for our vacation, it still turned out perfectly lovely, if chock full of pivots.

I highly recommend traveling with your mate before making any kind of bigger commitment. Testing the strength of your connection in this way is time well spent, even if things go to shit (maybe especially then). How you treat each other when stressed is an important factor in assessing the resilience of your bond because not every trip in life turns out to be the sunny paradise you expected.

# Love Maintenance Habits

Some people fall into the trap of thinking that marriage is all work, a drag, the old ball and chain. Their story is that once you are married, it's just a grind. You behave like married people – sex drops off, date nights become fewer and farther between, you fight over money or child rearing or who cleans the toilet. You live for nights out with your friends (because your spouse is not your friend). But dating is fun, exciting, thrilling because love is fresh and new and special. While dating, we are still wooing and being wooed. There is effort going on and interest in each other and fucking romance.

My husband and I are both committed romantics so we decided to never stop being boyfriend and girlfriend to each other. Our family thinks we are sappy and our teenagers roll their eyes a lot, but we don't care. Its not a huge amount of effort, any of these things we do for each other, but it keeps it fun. We have made a conscious decision to never stop seeing each other in that light, the light of early love. Ok, even I am cringing now at how cheesy this sounds, but it is totally true! It is vital to the survival of our relationship that we continue to make the effort to show  how important we are to each other. We have both had our share of challenges in life and are grateful for the love we have found. Here are some of our strategies to not fuck it up!

These habits are so deeply ingrained now that we don't even have to think about them all that hard anymore. They're just a part of our lifestyle. However, these aren't the only tools out there to keep a relationship strong and yours might look different than ours. That's okay. It's kind of like how they say you should pick exercises that you naturally like so that it will be easier to stick with them. Well, the same goes for developing loving habits with your partner. Pick stuff that you already enjoy doing—as long as your partner enjoys them, too—and repeat! Everybody wins. The bit about your partner feeling loved by these actions is really important to emphasize, because you could spend a lot of time and energy loving them in *your* way, but if it doesn't resonate with them, you might as well be pissing into the wind. So make sure that you're speaking *their* love language and not your own. If you're lucky like us, these will be the same, so no translation is necessary.

## Saying It Out Loud

Very early on our path together, and due to wounds and hurts that we'd sustained in other relationships, we made a solemn pact to always "Say it out loud." We both knew what it felt like to have our voices ignored or silenced to the point that we gave up even *trying* to talk to our partners. Neither one of us was interested in repeating that kind of hollow union, but we *did* have wounds and were afraid to hope that things could ever be different. And so giving each other the marching orders that we'd have to say difficult and even potentially explosive things out loud to each other went a long way to helping us be completely open with each other.

This type of unflinching honesty has steered us clear of many potential problems and misunderstandings, because we know that we're getting the straight story from each other without subterfuge of any sort. If one if us is feeling hurt or scared or uncertain or is questioning something, we just share it and take care of it. We don't hide our feelings from each other out of fear, shame, or anything else. But lest I oversell this as an easy endeavor, let me acknowledge that this *is* scary. It takes a lot of courage to be completely vulnerable with another person when you've been hurt in intimate relationships in the past. I am so glad that we were both willing to be brave and trust each other to be kind and receptive. It took courage to commit to this, and it was fucking terrifying at the beginning, but the payoff is worth it. It feels so safe to be able to talk about *anything*.

However, just because you can "say it out loud" doesn't necessarily mean that you should. It's not a blank check to go hog wild and spew out to your partner willy-nilly any and everything that comes to mind. Hear me out. Part of the art of relationships is recognizing that what, how and when something is said matters. Ask yourself: Is what I want to say meaningful? Is it kind? Is this the right time for my partner to hear this (if it is something potentially challenging)? Is it helpful? Honesty without consideration can be hurtful and damaging. So, go ahead, strive for "say it out loud" in your relationship, but proceed with care. Honesty doesn't happen in a vacuum and we all have tender hearts.

## Morning Check-Ins

At the beginning of each day, unless one of us has an extra early start, our routine goes something like this: I'm already awake (since I'm the early bird) and cuddled up with tea, dog, and crosswords in our morning spot, and maybe I'm even writing. He makes sure to give me sufficient time to wake up and enjoy some healthy solitude before settling in for a visit. When he comes down later, he gets his coffee and cozies into the couch across from me for a little chat.

Then we check in with each other, ask how each other slept, and share any news that might've come overnight. Next, we compare schedules for the day and sometimes the week ahead, too. We discuss what we're thinking of doing for dinner, and possibly engage in a little political roundup (we're in election season as I write this). Occasionally, we talk about work or family or stuff that we're going through—maybe insights we've had since we saw each other last the night before. It's a time and space for us to stay in touch and keep pace with each other's lives. We do this at other times of the day too, but starting the day together like this is an incredibly nice and enjoyable part of our routine, and so we make time for it whenever possible. You can borrow our routine anytime you like; it's highly recommended.

## Dive Bars

I'm going to use "dive bars" as code for our shared interests. We have other shared interests as well, but dive bars are a favorite. It also makes for a much more eye-catching title for this section!

A month into our romance, Steven set up a website for us to make content about our shared love of these kinds of places. Portlanddivebars.com was born in 2017 and became a creative outlet for us to share our experiences in the somewhat-seedier spaces populating our area. What started out as a fun, funny thing to do together has since grown into a living and breathing archive of almost 100 dive bars in our fair city! Plus, three published guidebooks—*Portland Dive Bar Passport, V*olume 1, 2 and 3 (and yes, that's a shameless plug). For us, it's just a fun thing to do together, but somehow it's also turned into a hyper-local microenterprise. Again, the universe is crazy with its tricks and twists.

We also love reading—especially educational and spiritual books and detective novels. He buys new and prefers hardcover, underlines as he reads, and keeps everything. I love borrowing paperbacks from the library or buying used, and then donating or passing on to others. Either way, it's fun to share reading recommendations with each other or discussing books that we've both read. It's like we've got our own mini book club with a membership of two!

Both of us grew up in the '80s which is a fun way to relate to one another. We can riff about cartoons, movies, laissez-faire parenting (to the extreme), snacks, banana seat bikes, and commercials. It's fun to reminisce with someone who lived through the same shit *you* did, and you don't have to explain every reference because they already know that Count Chocula cereal is fucking delicious, for example.

As mentioned a bit earlier, politics is another thing we enjoy following, although at times it makes us (okay me) cry. He's far better at remaining somewhat detached and seeing it as a sport rather than as evidence of the moral erosion of our nation. Nevertheless, it definitely gives us plenty to talk about!

Travel and exploring new places, especially beaches, is another shared interest. We're both curious by nature and enjoy learning about many things, but especially unique locales and people. One of our favorite things to do is get guidebooks prior to a trip and read all about where we're going. The anticipation is delicious!

Speaking of which, food is another big, shared interest, and it often guides our travel plans. We enjoy eating well, trying new restaurants and bars, and learning about the world through food. That love is expressed through different kinds of content we each make about our travels—I write stuff and Steven loves taking photographs and making videos (he even contributed a chapter to a textbook about food tourism!). And sometimes we collaborate. You can check out some of the content we've created together at our website (thisistraveltr easure.com). For example, we've posted articles, videos, and tons of photos online from our trips to Belize and Hollywood, among others. We make such a great team, and it's deliriously fun to be creative together.

Date Nights

Ah, the old classic! You may roll your eyes, but dedicating some regular time to being together is essential to a healthy relationship. Our attitude has always been this: we're still dating each other only we're married now! It doesn't have to be overly complicated. If you have low energy, limited time, and not a lot of funds, you can *still* do this. In fact, many times our "dates" are meeting up on the couch on Sunday afternoons to watch a movie with popcorn, or having cocktails and dinner at home. I cook, he mixes up the drinks, and we *always* agree on the music (generally Frank Sinatra).

He also still refers to me as his girlfriend, brings me flowers for no reason, and gazes at me adoringly while I whip up our meals. I buy him lots of butter and the right olives for his martinis, and I always compliment his outfits. Even though we're just at home, it still feels like special time together—maybe even sacred time. He's better at dressing up for our home events (he *does* love his outfits), but I try to at least put on a little perfume and lipstick, maybe some earrings, and a cute apron (he's made certain that I have quite a collection to choose from). We enjoy the subtle shift in atmosphere, and it feels like an occasion—not just any old Thursday night.

Celebrations

Honestly, we make a point of celebrating almost everything! Certainly the big stuff—birthdays, holidays, career wins—but also the little things like getting though a hard week or finishing a house project. It doesn't matter what it is—we'll find a way to glorify it!

One of our most enduring things to celebrate is the monthly anniversary of our first date. This means that on the 13$^{th}$ of every month (or close enough to it), you'll find us marking the occasion in some way. It started out a bit more ebullient with cards, flowers, and gifts, but now that we've just passed our 86$^{th}$ monthly anniversary (!), we've toned it down a bit—usually just an exchange of cards and a date night. It's some silly fun that we agreed that we'd keep up with until it started to become a chore or lost its shine. And it still hasn't. It still feels meaningful.

I think that this and everything else we choose to celebrate is significant to us, because we've both endured our share of losses in life. We both painfully know that life can be cut short at any time. This is why we choose to enjoy and appreciate and give thanks for whatever time we have together, because you just don't know how much time you've got.

## Pebbling

I love this concept. Never heard of it? "Pebbling" is small ways of showing affection that may serve as a bridge to deeper conversations (so says Psychology Today magazine). The term was apparently derived from the behavior of penguin couples—they bring each other little stones (or pebbles) to show devotion (which is absolutely darling—picture it!).

We do this a ton on social media. Every morning, I wake up to a slew of fun TikToks he's sent me over night, and I respond with appropriate emojis. I forward him news stories and cocktail recipes I think he might like. He takes pictures of funny grocery store items or kitchen gadgets because I adore them, and also bananas because I loathe them (he likes to stir me up). I leave him love notes on his desk when he's working late. These are all examples of pebbling—just little touches that let us know that we're thinking about one another. If it's good enough for the penguins, it definitely is for us.

## Affection & Loving Words

Speaking of words, we're a touchy couple and we both thrive when given words of affirmation. I don't think that a day has gone by without a hug or a kiss or an "I love you" being exchanged. And I *so* love giving him spontaneous bear hugs in the kitchen, grabbing his cute butt, and telling him how good he smells. And how wise and insightful and kind and caring he is. He ogles me (in a good way, obviously) and tells me that I'm a good mom and beautiful and smart and an excellent writer. Words matter. So does touch.

The foot rubs may not be as frequent as once before, but the cool thing is that now I have no reticence about asking for them. In past relationships, I felt like asking for what I wanted or needed was a burden to my partner, and if and when my request was granted, timely payback was expected. Give me a break. I'm not a "taker" at heart, and so it's honestly difficult for me to ask for things, but to be treated like someone who had to be monitored for abusing kindness was really disheartening for me. Just a reminder to all those in love land: chances are that you overvalue what *you* give and undervalue what *they* give. Do your best to throw out the scorecard, relinquish your role as the "fair police," and give with an open hand and heart in ways that are meaningful to your partner. It all usually works out over time. But remember—the path of life is uneven. One of you may be going through a rough patch for a while and have greater needs, but then the other will certainly have their time of trials later. Give because you love them—not with expectation of repayment or of evening the score. Also, err on the side of saying "I love you." Because not saying (or hearing) it enough is *awful*.

Banter

Merriam-Webster's definition of banter is "good-natured teasing or exchanging of clever remarks," and boy do we enjoy this! I'm smiling to myself just thinking about our schtick with each other. The content varies, but it might start off with him asking if we have any pickles, me saying yes, him looking in the fridge and not finding any, then me going to the fridge and plucking out three different jars of them—plus two from the pantry—and then him buying more pickles (or threatening to do so to wind me up). It's just silly fun that we have with each other's quirks.

It would be easy to let these quirks become sore spots and for the banter to become hard-edged teasing—especially when you don't have a "say it out loud" clause in place. Thank god we do, because we're both quirky as hell! But we kind of revel in it. He's a packrat (as previously detailed), has way too many shirts of the same color, leaves his coffee spoons and loose change all over the house, and the inside of his car looks like a bomb went off. I have an aversion to sunglasses worn inside, sleep with way too many pillows and can't seem to get my laundry out of the dryer in a timely fashion to save my life. I also make it a rule to buy house brands for most stuff because they're the same thing as name brands only cheaper (he does not agree), go to great lengths to repurpose leftovers and can't *stand* suitcases on the bed (do you know the germs that thing has seen? Filth!). We've chosen to laugh together about these things instead of getting all pissy about them. And if any quirk ever becomes problematic or if the banter veers into open-wound territory, we fall back on the "say it out loud" rule. But the sparring sure is a hoot!

## Texts

When we first got together, he used to drive me crazy by texting me his every waking movement. And then a funny thing happened: I actually came to like it, and now I look forward to his "pointless" missives. He doesn't necessarily need or expect me to reply, and so there's no pressure. He just wants to share his day with me and let me know that he's thinking about me. It makes me feel included on his daily adventures. Another thing he does is message me when he's on his way home, whether it's from the grocery store, across the bridge, or across the state. He actually sends me a screenshot of the map with his expected arrival time. How sweet is *that*? I never asked for it—it's just something thoughtful that he started all on his own. I need to strive harder to do the same, but it's still an aspirational habit for me at this point. But I am great at texting him whenever I'm having good and fuzzy feelings about him. He really enjoys it when I randomly surprise him with those sweet words. And I know that he does, that's why I do it. And because I just plain want to express out loud the joy I feel being with him, whenever I feel it. This good man was long dreamed of and hard won! Thank god I waited for him.

<u>Cheering Each Other On</u>

Since we're both creative, self-employed people, we don't have a lot of external guidance or guardrails keeping us on track. While this is a fantastic blessing—freedom!—it also has a sharp side to it. We have to rely on ourselves to figure out what to create, what the deadline is, and then make it happen. There is no boss demanding accountability; we have to provide that for ourselves. And with creative pursuits like writing, sometimes the motivation is just plain MIA. And *that's* when the worry sets in: *Is it ever going to come back? Will I ever have another good idea or take another picture? Will my video skills improve? Will I ever finish this fucking book?* That's where we pick each other up, dust ourselves off, and give a little pep talk. It's not just blowing smoke, either—we genuinely believe in each other's work and make a point of saying it out loud. Frequently.

Story time:

I have always loved cooking, but for most of my life didn't see it much beyond a fun and functional hobby to express my creativity. To me, it is both relaxing and stimulating. At the best of times I have that delicious feeling of being in "the flow" where I don't have to think hard about what I am doing but everything is just clicking right into place anyway. It feels like I am in my element. Friends and family benefit from my skills in the kitchen as well, and have not been reserved in their praise (which embarrasses me, I'm still not very comfortable taking compliments).

At one point in the past, I had a friend encourage me to produce and sell a small food item that she thought was especially good and marketable on a small, farmer's market kind of scale. When I shyly shared this idea with my then partner, he snorted and said "You'll never get rich doing *that*." Proverbial lead balloon. I remember feeling pretty crushed. Not so much because making and selling that particular thing was my dream, but because my partner didn't support me pursuing something that touched that quiet part of me that was important to who I am. The part that didn't dare hope to dream about the possibility of pursuing a creative life. He didn't have to believe in the profitability of the proposed product, but he sure as shit could have believed in me.

Steven tells me that I can do it (whatever "it" happens to be at that moment)and truly believes in my capacity to pursue my dreams (even when I don't). I try to do the same for him. I review his work, edit, encourage and give honest feedback with a healthy dose of "you got this." We spend hours together plotting the path of our dreams. We both see the wisdom of small steps in the right direction. These add up over time and who knows where they might lead. If you don't ever turn yourself in the right direction, you can be sure chances are slim you will ever get anywhere good. Having him coaching and cheering me on in big stuff (massive career change) as well as small stuff (trying a new recipe, wearing a new hat) makes me feel empowered. Small wins are recognized just as eagerly as major achievements in our house, and *this* is how we keep going.

## Take Care of Yourself

We both recognize the necessity of identifying and managing our own needs to maximize our wellbeing. Even though it doesn't come easy, we encourage each other to do things for ourselves so that we can both be physically and emotionally healthy for each other.

One way that worked for us introverts was figuring out how to be together *and* apart at the same time. We both need regular doses of solitude to rest and recharge and be our best selves. We stunned ourselves by realizing we could be home together and peacefully working for long stretches in different rooms of the house without one or the other of us feeling lonely or neglected. Our sleep patterns sort of organically evolved to where we now have different bedtimes, which effectively gives him time alone at night and me time alone in the morning. We also use separate comforters so that we can both wrap up like burritos at night. And for those of you who wonder how this arrangement affects our sex life, remember—we're self-employed, and so any part of the day is fair game for lovin'. And a well-rested, fulfilled partner tends to be far more available for such activities!

# True Love

So there you have it—all my tried, tested, and very true secrets to finding real love and *staying* in love. You breakup properly (with whoever your Mr. Wrong is at the time), you heal your wounds, you create a life that you love, and *then* you start looking for partner to share it with. While you're dating, you avoid being desperate, know your own value, and are stingy with second dates, but *always* kind when turning people down. You are clear about who you're looking for so that you can spot them when they eventually appear in your dating landscape.

Repeat, repeat, repeat.

Until you don't *have* to repeat it anymore.

Because true love *will* come and at that point, you'll be thankful for each and every Rude Dude, Mean Dad, and Fish Farm Guy who ever walked out of your life. And you'll smile, knowing that they all played significant parts on your fraught (but temporary, I promise) journey to find Mr. Right.

You might shudder a bit, looking back. But you'll definitely smile too.

Because it was never about them anyway, was it? It was always about your happy ending—they just helped you eventually get there, one desperate date at a time.

# Favorite Bits of Wisdom Gained Through Dating

Dating is educational and so are relationships. You learn a lot about yourself and what you want and need (and what you *don't* want and need). Lots of lessons in love to be learned out there, here are some of mine that I lovingly pass on to you:

- Be diligent with dating, not desperate. Desperation is a very effective love repellant.

- If you aren't pleased with the quality of dates or relationships you're attracting, have a look inside. Your childhood wounds might be holding you back.

- The relationships you were exposed to in childhood influence the ones in your adulthood.

- You don't have to be completely healed before you go looking for love, but at least be on the road to getting there!

- You'll grow on this journey—wherever it leads—and

it'll *always* be worthwhile.

- Finding love is a process, so be patient and let it unfold organically. And have fun with it!

- People lie on the internet. It's inevitable, because we all have soft spots that make us feel inadequate. Keep your guard up.

- Never chat for too long online. Meet in person as soon as possible lest you develop unrealistic expectations.

- Don't go out on that first date if there are even *minor* red flags or if you're not feeling it. There are plenty of prospective partners out there. Trust your gut!

- Be stingy with second dates. A second occasion with you is a privilege.

- There is someone out there who will fit you. And more than one. Don't buy into that bullshit of there only being one true love for each of us.

- Try not to be discouraged if someone rejects you (unless you've got work to do on improving yourself that you're letting slip!)

- Dating is as much about getting to know yourself as it is about getting to know the other person.

- "Fit" is the most important thing. You gotta fit.

- Because with the right fit, the relationship doesn't feel like work (most of the time).

- You want passion, but not *just* passion.

- There's absolutely nothing wrong with having a Mr. Right Now.

- Go for partners who can communicate directly. No BS.

- Confidence is wildly attractive.

- Don't let *anyone* shame you for who you are.

- Don't be with someone who isn't kind to their own kids. How on earth will they treat *you*?

- Stay mindful of how what you're doing in your love life affects the other important people in your life (especially the kids).

- There is benefit to allowing some time to pass before making any big decisions in a new relationship. See how it wears over a little bit of time. Its ok to be convinced in the beginning that you have found true love and enjoy that feeling to the fullest! Just don't rush into any life changing decisions too soon.

- Play the long game with your budding relationship, especially when there are kids involved on either side. There's no need to rush. The kids will do better if you move things along on *their* timetable (which may be entirely different from yours).

- Give with an open heart, and don't keep score.

- Always speak respectfully to each other, no matter what.

- Celebrate. Frequently.

- Make an effort to enjoy the simple pleasures. These are what sustain a great love; more so than a few grand gestures here and there.

- Remember that you're on the same side with your partner—especially in the face of adversity.

- Be really good friends to each other.

- Always look for the good in each other and cheer each other on.

- Say it out loud.

- Great relationships require bravery—it takes a lot of courage to be vulnerable.

- Never stop growing.

- The right partner will support you and encourage you to keep growing—always.

- Sometimes, when you let go is when the thing you want most appears. Remember—the universe is crazy this way!

- One more time: The "break-up and make-up" cycle is best avoided at all costs. It *never* works.

# 13-Steps to Finding True Love

A condensed version of my successful dating strategy for those who want the highlights:

1. Spend time on your own after your last break up to grieve, heal, and learn.

2. Figure out how to achieve a level of comfort when it comes to being alone.

3. Create a life worth living—even without a partner. (This and number 2 above help prevent desperate dating.)

4. Make a detailed list of who you're looking for once you feel ready to date. You're ready when you have an open mind and heart—no bitterness or other unhealthy emotions.

5. Put some thought into creating a dating profile with solid pictures (and have it vetted by your most honest friend!).

6. Scroll and swipe away! Dating is a numbers game, so cast a wide net and start making contacts with people who look interesting.

7. Make plans for an in-person first date early in the getting-to-know-you process.

8. Devise a go-to first date outfit that you feel good in. (Steve Jobs did turtlenecks every day, and *he* was a success. Just sayin'.)

9. Identify a comfortable place to meet first dates—preferably close to home and quiet enough for chatting.

10. Put together a list of a few creative, getting-to-know-you questions in case conversation stalls. Pluck up your courage and take comfort in the fact that if the date goes badly, you never have to see them again!

11. Create a polished and kind sentence to decline a second date when needed. (Use liberally!)

12. Revise your desired list frequently as you date to distill what you want in a relationship.

13. Have patience and hold out for a person who fits. Take breaks from dating as needed. Prepare yourself—this may take some time and a *lot* of dates, but it's so very worth it.

# My Honest-to-God List

As mentioned earlier in the book, this right here is the actual list I put together of everything I was looking for in a long-term love before I met him. Remember—it doesn't hurt to ask for whatever you want, so make the picture as complete as possible. You may not get your entire list (though it's possible—I did!), but hopefully most of it.

- Kind

- Intelligent

- Motivated but also easygoing

- Funny and likes to laugh

- Creative

- Tall (!), dark, and handsome

- When I am with him I feel understood, cherished, safe and protected

- Family oriented

- Big, burly and furry teddy bear of a man

- Self-aware and introspective

- Good conversationalist, likes to talk deep

- Lifelong learner, always trying to grow

- Loves to read

- Likes me just the way I am, but also helps me to grow however is important to me

- Enjoys travel

- Doesn't take himself too seriously

- Big-hearted and generous

- Unfailingly supportive of my hopes and dreams

- Comforts me when I need it

- Quirky and interesting

I got everything on my list and more, except for tall (but hey—tall, schmall...who cares? How shallow would I be if that were a dealbreaker?)

# Playlist (Shared on Spotify)

Tired of Being Alone – Al Green

I Wanna Be Your Boyfriend – Ramones

You Sexy Thing – Hot Chocolate

Every Little Thing She Does is Magic – The Police

Crazy Love – Van Morrison

I've Got the World on a String – Frank Sinatra

Ain't That a Kick in the Head – Dean Martin

Gimme! Gimme! Gimme! – ABBA

Somebody to Love – Jefferson Airplane

Somebody to Love – Queen

Something Just Like This – The Chainsmokers & Coldplay

The Night We Met – Lord Huron

Love Story – Taylor Swift

Hot Stuff – Donna Summer

What I Like About You – The Romantics

Hot N Cold – Katy Perry

Don't Go Breaking My Heart – Elton John & Kiki Dee

Bad Romance – Lady Gaga

I Will Survive – Gloria Gaynor

When I'm 64 – The Beatles

I Can Make You a Man – Tim Curry

3AM – Matchbox Twenty

You Are the Best Thing – Ray LaMontagne

When a Man Loves a Woman – Percy Sledge

My Baby Just Cares for Me – Nina Simone

I Melt with You – Modern English

Unchained Melody – The Righteous Brothers

Head Over Heels – The Go-Go's

Only Wanna Be with You – Hootie & the Blowfish

Wonderful Tonight – Eric Clapton

Let's Get It On – Marvin Gaye

Can't Get Enough of Your Love – Barry White

You Can't Hurry Love – The Supremes

Is This Love – Bob Marley and the Wailers

Heartbreak Beat – Psychedelic Furs

Better Man – Pearl Jam

Should I Stay Or Should I Go? – The Clash

Suspicious Minds – Elvis Presley

The One I Love – REM

Tainted Love – Soft Cell

Think – Aretha Franklin

A Little Respect – Erasure

This Charming Man – The Smiths

Signed, Sealed, Delivered – Stevie Wonder

*At Last – Etta James

*_This_ is our song. _Sigh._

# Movies That Influenced This Book

I was influenced by all these films and all for different reasons. Some are about wanting love, finding love or losing love, while others are about being happy (or unhappy) in love or alone. There are good examples, bad examples and just plain weird examples of love in all its different forms. This movie selection demonstrates the width and breadth of what love is, isn't and, most importantly, what it can be. I sheepishly admit that I do love love!

An Affair to Remember

The American President

Under The Tuscan Sun

A Good Year

Pillow Talk

The Notebook

Mamma Mia

Titanic

The Saint

The Lover

Grease

Sense and Sensibility

Amelie

Love Actually

So I Married an Ax Murderer

Moonstruck

Age of Innocence

Doctor Zhivago

Gone with the Wind

Singles

Better Off Dead

Edward Scissorhands

Bridget Jones' Diary

Like Water for Chocolate

Sabrina

How Stella Got Her Groove Back

Love Story

The Wedding Banquet

Dangerous Liaisons

Kramer vs. Kramer

Fatal Attraction

# Foods That Helped Me Write This Love Story

Martinis

Risotto Milanese

Butter-basted ribeye steaks

Cambazola cheese and cornichons

Joann's Marinara

Roasted tofu

Lemon Lima Beans

Scalloped Potatoes

Jalapeno poppers

Chicken pot pie

# The Team Behind This Book

Christina Beck

Cody Brown

Rebecca Heigl

Nash Nelson

Nora Nelson

Zack Nelson

Rob Peace

Darlene Pruessmann

Zac Shomler

My therapist

My husband, Steven Shomler

KC Shomler has always gravitated toward the less-traveled road with the better view. That approach to life bleeds into her writing; whether about her life path or the literal paths between the dive bars she so dearly loves, she writes about it all.

KC lives in southwestern Washington state with her cute husband and a tiny dog with an outsized ego who runs the house. She is the author of *Falling Out of Love with My Career* which is her personal story about giving up her healthcare career when it no longer fit. She also writes more light-hearted material, including the *Portland Dive Bar Passport* series of books which offer self-guided tours of (and highly opinionated looks at) the seedier side of Portland, Oregon.

*